AUGUSTO PINOCHET'S

CHILE

DIANA CHILDRESS

TWENTY-FIRST CENTURY BOOKS   MINNEAPOLIS

For Jo, a friend indeed.

Consultant: Mark Ensalaco, Ph.D., Raymond A. Roesch Chair in the Social Sciences, University of Dayton, Ohio

Note: Chileans follow the Spanish custom of using two surnames. To limit confusion, only one surname has been used throughout this book.

Twenty-First Century Books
A division of Lerner Publishing Group, Inc.
241 First Avenue North
Minneapolis, MN 55401 U.S.A.

Website address: www.lernerbooks.com

Library of Congress Cataloging-in-Publication Data

Childress, Diana.
   Augusto Pinochet's Chile / by Diana Childress.
      p.   cm. — (Dictatorships)
   Includes bibliographical references and index.
   ISBN 978–0–8225–8667–8 (lib. bdg. : alk. paper)
      1. Chile—History—1973–1988. 2. Chile—History—Coup d'état, 1973.
   3. Pinochet Ugarte, Augusto. I. Title.
   F3100.C436 2009
   983.06'5—dc22   2008000403

Manufactured in the United States of America
1 2 3 4 5 6 – DP – 14 13 12 11 10 09

CONTENTS

EL ONCE

ON TUESDAY, SEPTEMBER 11, 1973, two jets whizzed across blue skies above Santiago, the capital of Chile. It was almost noon. Late-winter sun glinted on silver wings as the planes soared over the broad valley. Snowcapped peaks overlooked office towers, and homes spread out on the plain below.

The jets streaked toward La Moneda Palace in the heart of the city. A grand old Spanish colonial building, La Moneda had housed the offices of democratically elected presidents of Chile for 130 years. Chile's president, Salvador Allende, was inside.

Diving steeply, the jets fired a load of rockets. A screeching whistle sliced the air, high at first, then lower and lower, disappearing with a loud boom. Well-aimed missiles struck the north side of the palace. They shattered windows and set fire to curtains. The jets rose, circled around, and bombed the palace again and again

SMOKE POURS FROM THE WINDOWS OF LA MONEDA PALACE IN SANTIAGO, CHILE.

Chilean Air Force planes attacked the palace during the 1973 military coup that overthrew President Salvador Allende.

and again, until flames lapped the thick old walls and black smoke darkened the sun.

No foreign enemy was striking at Chile. The jets belonged to the Chilean Air Force. Surrounding the palace, Chilean Army troops and tanks were poised for a ground assault. Coordinating the attack from an army communications facility on the outskirts of Santiago was the commander in chief of Chile's army, General Augusto Pinochet. "The attack on La Moneda must start at eleven on the dot because this rooster isn't going to give up," he ordered.

The "rooster" Pinochet was referring to was President Salvador Allende. President Allende had been elected three years earlier to lead Chile's democratic government for a six-year term.

"Attack La Moneda now! Hard!" Pinochet barked over communications lines set up among the separate command posts of the military leaders who plotted the coup. The harshest and most rigid voice in the discussions recorded that day, Pinochet was opposed to any concessions. "Unconditional surrender! No negotiating! Unconditional surrender!" he shouted at the others. When a naval officer proposed that Allende should be allowed to leave Chile, Pinochet relented. "But the plane falls out of the sky while flying," he added. The naval officer assumed that was a joke and laughed.

By nightfall on *el once* (the eleventh, in Spanish), as Chileans speak of that fateful September 11, President Allende was dead. Four men in uniform appeared on national television to introduce themselves as a junta (a group that seizes power and takes control of a government). They were Pinochet; General Gustavo Leigh, who had recently been appointed commander of the Chilean Air Force; Admiral José Toribio Merino, who had seized command of the Chilean Navy; and General César Mendoza, who had taken command of the carabineros, or national police.

It was "patriotic duty," Pinochet proclaimed, that impelled the armed forces to overthrow the Allende administration. With chilling bluntness, he announced that new ministers and governors would be appointed from the military. The junta would be responsible for all branches of government, he continued, and the Congress would be suspended until further notice. Few suspected then that they were witnessing the beginning of a brutal dictatorship that would hold power over Chile for the next seventeen years.

PERU

BOLIVIA

*PACIFIC
OCEAN*

Arica

Pisagua

Iquique

Calama

Antofagasta

ARGENTINA

CHILE

JUAN
FERNÁNDEZ
ISLANDS

Mapocho River

Quillota

Valparaíso

San Antonio

Santiago

CENTRAL VALLEY

Talcahuano

Concepción

Bío Bío River

**AUGUSTO
PINOCHET'S
CHILE**

**SOUTH
AMERICA**

*PACIFIC
OCEAN*

CHILE

*ATLANTIC
OCEAN*

N

ATACAMA DESERT

ANDES MOUNTAINS

Miles

0   200   400

0   200   400   600

Kilometers

*Strait of
Magellan*

TIERRA DEL FUEGO
(ARGENTINA)

*ATLANTIC
OCEAN*

**TIERRA
DEL FUEGO
(CHILE)**

Beagle Channel

Drake Passage

THE NATION

MILITARY ATTACKS ON THE PRESIDENCY and takeovers by a junta of officers were not common occurrences in Chile. "Coups d'etat do not happen in Chile," Pinochet had told a meeting of right-wing newspaper editors two years earlier, in December 1971. At that time, the journalists were trying to goad the army into taking violent action against President Allende.

Chile had a reputation for stable government. Rule by peacefully elected presidents had been almost continuous since its independence from Spain in the early nineteenth century. Before 1973 this peace was interrupted by brief periods of unrest only three times. Chileans prided themselves on their long history of democracy, so unlike that of many of their Latin American neighbors.

Chile's relatively peaceful history may be partly due to the country's geography. Wedged between the tall, rugged Andes

Mountains and the vast Pacific Ocean, Chile was long isolated, fenced off by deserts to the north, mountains to the east, the ocean to the west, and the treacherous ice of the Antarctic to the south. "The worst-located and worst-shaped nation on the planet" a writer from neighboring Argentina once said.

Chileans refer to their skinny country as "a long and narrow sash of land." It is 2,600 miles (4,200 kilometers) long and on average only about 90 miles (145 km) wide. It extends across thirty-eight degrees of latitude—from the tropics in the north to the icy waters of Drake Passage, off Cape Horn in the south. If Chile were lined up with the western coast of North America, it would reach from the southern tip of Baja California, Mexico, to Juneau, Alaska.

At the center of the country, between the Andes and a coastal range, lies the Central Valley. This is a series of hills and valleys formed by rivers flowing from the Andes to the sea. Here is the heartland of Chile. Most Chileans live in this region of fertile well-watered highlands, enjoying a climate similar to that of California.

The capital and largest city of Chile, Santiago, lies at the northern end of the Central Valley. Almost one-third of Chile's population inhabits this sprawling city. Only 75 miles (121 km) to the northeast, Valparaíso, the principal port and second-largest urban area, spreads out on hills overlooking a large bay. At the southern edge of the Central Valley region, 300 miles (480 km) from Santiago, is Chile's third-largest urban area, Concepción. Situated on the Bío-Bío River, Concepción and its nearby port, Talcahuano, form the gateway to southern Chile.

EARLY SETTLEMENT

The first Chileans, like all Native Americans, descended from groups of Stone Age hunters who migrated from Asia to the Americas twenty thousand or more years ago. By the time Europeans began exploring the area in the sixteenth century, about one million people lived on the strip of land along the Pacific coast. Many of the people living in the northern part had been conquered by the Incas of Peru in the fifteenth century. But hunter-gatherers living in central and southern areas had resisted Inca armies. They called themselves Mapuche: People of the Land. The Incas called them Araucanians: Indomitable Ones.

Europeans first saw Chile in 1520 from the three ships Ferdinand Magellan sailed around the tip of South America. Thirteen years later, Francisco Pizarro and his small band of Spanish conquistadors

The Spanish admired the fighting spirit of the Mapuche. In the late 1500s, a Spanish soldier-poet, Alonso de Ercilla, composed an epic poem about the conquest of Chile, *La Araucana*. In it he depicted Mapuche leaders as heroes.

invaded Peru and toppled the wealthy Inca Empire. In 1536 another Spaniard, Diego de Almagro, hoping to discover yet more riches, led an expedition southward. He crossed the Atacama Desert, the driest desert on Earth, and reached the Central Valley of Chile, but Mapuche warriors soon drove the explorers back to Peru.

Pedro de Valdivia led a second Spanish expedition to Chile in 1540. He founded the city of Santiago in 1541. The Mapuche again fought fiercely against the Spanish settlers and killed Valdivia in battle in 1553. Spanish soldiers, however, gradually pushed the indigenous (local) people south of the Bío-Bío River and gave up trying to conquer them. The Bío-Bío became a long-standing hostile frontier between Spanish Chile and what the Spanish called Araucania.

The Spaniards who settled in the Central Valley converted the people they conquered to Christianity and put them to work tilling the soil and panning the rivers for gold. As the Spanish invaders took over their land and their lives, the indigenous cultures of northern and central Chile were slowly wiped out. European diseases, such as smallpox and typhus—to which the Native Americans had no resistance—killed off an estimated 80 percent of the original population. Indigenous cultures were lost as they were assimilated into European culture and as Spanish settlers and indigenous people had mestizo (mixed) children together.

COLONIAL RULE

For almost three centuries, Chile remained a minor province of Spain's American empire. After panning all the gold out of the rivers, the colonists turned to ranching and growing wheat, exporting meat, leather, and flour to the richer Spanish colony in Peru. American-born settlers of Spanish descent, called *criollos* (Creoles), owned huge estates and gave themselves aristocratic titles. At the head of the colony, however, was the governor and, to advise him, an *audiencia* (audience, or tribunal) made up of judges and church officials. They were all *peninsulares* (native-born Spaniards from the Iberian Peninsula) appointed by Spanish authorities. Although criollos could not hold high office, they participated in the local politics of the *cabildos* (town councils) and sometimes married into the ruling class. At the bottom of the class system, mestizos and conquered Native Americans supported the colony with their labor. Unlike many Spanish colonies, Chile did not import large numbers of African slaves. About four thousand slaves were freed when Chile abolished slavery in 1823.

Virtually all settlers were Spanish or of Spanish descent, and all were Roman Catholics, the only religion allowed. Many of Chile's ruling officials were military leaders, and the colony had a standing army to deal with Mapuche attacks. To the settlers, the military stood for law and order.

Although colonial Chile was a relatively poor and remote outpost, a few non-Spanish adventurers made their way there. One was Ambrose O'Higgins, who emigrated from Ireland to South America, joined the Spanish army as an engineer, and rose first to head Chile's colonial government, then later to become viceroy (appointed governor) of Peru. An obscure French trader, Guillaume Pinochet, arrived from Brittany (in northwestern France) about 1720, settled in Concepción, and raised a large family.

INDEPENDENCE FROM SPAIN

In the late eighteenth century, ideas of independence that swept through North America and France also spread to South America. Like the founders of the United States, a number of South American leaders urged colonists to rebel against the distant government that gave them little say in how their colonies were run. In Chile, Bernardo O'Higgins (1778–1842), the son of Ambrose, played a major role in plotting the overthrow of Spanish rule.

In 1808 French emperor Napoleon Bonaparte marched into Spain and put his brother on the Spanish throne. This gave Spanish America an additional cause for rebellion. Even moderates, who like North American Tories preferred a monarchy to democracy, did not want a French king. Many who joined the rebellions still wanted a strong, authoritarian government, not democracy.

Chile declared its independence on September 18, 1810. It chose a six-person junta to govern the colony until the rightful Spanish king was restored to the throne of Spain. The revolutionaries soon defeated Spanish forces stationed in Chile. But the struggle for independence was not over. When the British defeated Napoleon in 1814, the Spanish monarchy was restored. Spain launched a campaign to win back its rebellious empire. Latin Americans, however, were too caught up in the struggle to abandon it. Chile finally secured its independence from Spain in 1818.

A NEW CONSTITUTION

Bernardo O'Higgins was named supreme director of the new country. Five years later, when he proposed a new constitution that would give him ten additional years in office, Congress forced him to abdicate. Over the next decade, Chilean leaders wrote and rewrote constitutions, adopting and then rejecting various political structures. Finally, in 1833, they agreed on a constitution that remained in effect for almost a century.

The constitution of 1833 was masterminded by a young businessman turned politician, Diego Portales. He wanted to ensure that wealthy landowners like himself would control the government. Voting was limited to men over twenty-five (over twenty-one if married) who owned property. Presidents were allowed to serve two five-year terms and had broad powers. The president could appoint provincial governors and influence congressional elections by issuing lists of approved candidates to his appointees. Voting was not by secret ballot. Voters were often intimidated, temporarily arrested, or bribed to vote "correctly" by governors wanting to retain their positions.

DIEGO PORTALES WAS BORN in Santiago in 1793. He studied law and helped write the conservative Chilean constitution of 1833.

Portales never ran for public office, but he was both the minister of interior and external relations and the minister of war and the navy. He used his cabinet posts to restore many practices initiated by the Spaniards when they ruled. Catholicism remained the official religion of Chile. Portales reintroduced primogeniture, a system of inheritance that allows only the eldest son to inherit a family's property. In this way, large estates would not be divided into smaller plots inherited by several children. By preventing the breakup of large estates, Portales ensured there would always be a class of rich landholders to provide political leaders. Portales also strengthened and organized the military, dismissing officers who disagreed with his conservative politics. For several years, Portales was a virtual dictator of Chile, until his opponents assassinated him in 1837.

A MODEL OF STABILITY

The constitution of 1833 introduced a long period of political stability in Chile. Four presidents held office over the next four decades, followed by three who served single five-year terms. As the nineteenth century progressed, Chilean politics gradually grew more liberal. A multi-party system developed. A new electoral law in 1874 made literacy, not property ownership, the only qualification for voting (although the vote was still limited to men).

This was a time of economic progress for Chile as well. Under Spanish rule, Chile could only trade with Spain on Spanish terms. With colonial trade restrictions ended, commerce flourished. Ships from Great Britain, France, and the United States called at Chilean ports. Exports of copper, silver, and wheat enriched the upper class. New inventions such as steamships, railways, and the telegraph improved transportation and communications. Mining for coal, silver, copper, and nitrates expanded.

Chilean entrepreneurs moved beyond the border to develop mines in southern Peru and eastern Bolivia. In 1879, when Peru canceled contracts with Chilean companies, Chile declared war. Chile's defeat of its two northern neighbors in the War of the Pacific (1879–1883) added one-third more land to its territory. Bolivia lost its access to the sea, and Chile gained a greater portion of the Atacama Desert, with its rich sources of nitrate and copper—at a time when nitrate was heavily used as a fertilizer.

After the war, Chilean armies turned south and conquered the

CHILEAN SOLDIERS ATTACK THE COMBINED FORCES OF PERU AND BOLIVIA in the War of the Pacific. In this battle at Tacna, Peru, in 1880, the Chilean force outnumbered the Peruvian and Bolivian army by five thousand fighters.

Mapuche, who were still fighting against Chilean expansion into Araucania. Having lost their independence, the Mapuche withdrew to territories assigned to them by the Chilean government.

CONFLICT AND CHANGE

In 1891 a struggle between the presidency and the Congress led to a brief civil war. Conservative members of Congress opposed the liberal policies of President José Manuel Balmaceda. Aided by the Chilean navy, rebellious Congress members sailed to the northern port of Iquique. They mobilized nitrate workers there into an army, seized control of nitrate revenues to finance their cause, and secured help from British companies in the area. After seven months of war, the congressional forces marched triumphantly into Santiago. Balmaceda, refusing to surrender or go into exile, committed suicide.

For the next thirty years, Chile was a parliamentary republic—a government in which many of the usual presidential powers of government are carried out by members of the legislature. The press at one point complained of "the most reckless anarchy, produced by the irresponsible dictatorship of some 150 congressmen," but up until 1924, the government of Chile was stable.

A NEW CENTURY

In the late nineteenth century, Marxist ideas of workers' rights spread across the world. Workers and peasants revolted in Russia in 1905 and in Mexico five years later. Workers in Chile were also growing resentful of wealthy landholders and merchants who had run Chilean society virtually unchallenged since colonial times. The workers organized labor unions to improve wages and working conditions. But when they went on strike, the government called out the army. In 1903 one hundred striking port workers were killed in Valparaíso. An even worse massacre occurred four years later in Iquique, when troops with machine guns attacked thousands of striking nitrate miners and their families. The first Chilean political party embracing Marxist ideas, the Socialist Workers Party, was formed in 1912. It later became the Communist Party.

The technological developments of the twentieth century brought new challenges to the republic. When German scientists discovered a process for making artificial nitrates, Chile's nitrate industry suffered. And when the United States completed construction of the Panama Canal in 1914, fewer ships from Europe and the eastern coast of the Americas traveled the long and dangerous route around South America to the Pacific Ocean. Ships no longer needed to stop for supplies at Chile's ports. A slowdown in shipping due to the dangers of World War I (1914–1918) put a further crimp in Chile's foreign trade.

The economic setbacks affected wealthy Chileans less than they did the middle and working classes. The upper class owned all the best agricultural land. They also owned the factories that expanded manufacturing within Chile. The wealthy built mansions in Santiago, took long tours of Europe, and enjoyed newfangled inventions such as the telephone and automobiles. New technology, which improved copper mining processes, attracted U.S. companies to Chile.

MARXISM

Karl Marx (1818–1883) was a German economist and philosopher whose writings developed the underlying ideas of modern Communism and Socialism. His *Communist Manifesto*, written with Friedrich Engels in 1848, declared that all history is the history of class struggles. They saw the struggle of their time as being one between capitalists who controlled manufacturing, trade, government, and culture and workers whose labor gave capitalists economic power. If workers, who outnumbered capitalists, recognized where their true interests lay, they could overthrow Capitalism and create a Socialist society, where everyone's needs would be met. Marx called this goal Communism. The famous closing line of the *Manifesto* urged global revolution: "Workers of all lands, unite!"

Marx's theories had a great influence on workers and intellectuals in Europe, among them Vladimir Ilyich Lenin (1870–1924). In 1917 Lenin organized the Russian Communist Party and the Marxist government of Russia. In 1922 he reached an agreement with several smaller communist-led neighboring republics to form the Union of Soviet Socialist Republics (USSR), also known as the Soviet Union. Communist Party rule prevailed in the USSR until 1991.

Communist movements developed in many other countries as well. After World War II (1939–1945), the USSR established Communist governments in Eastern Europe and North Korea. Yugoslavia and Albania also formed Communist regimes independent of the Soviet Union. In 1949 a Communist movement under the leadership of Mao Zedong won control of China. In some African countries, Communists helped oust colonial rule. Fidel Castro brought Communism to Cuba in 1959.

Although many Communist countries have a totalitarian government ruled by a single party or dictator, some democratic countries, such as Chile, have Communist parties as part of a multi-party system. These Communist parties focus on social issues and workers' rights, not the violent overthrow of capitalism and the establishment of one-party rule.

The middle and working classes were harder hit. New processing methods for copper meant fewer jobs for Chile's miners, and reduced trade meant less work for farmhands. Unemployed workers crowded into city slums looking for jobs. There were frequent demonstrations, such as the one-day general strike in 1919 when one hundred thousand teachers, engineers, and health workers marched through Santiago demanding lower prices. Even the right-wing newspapers complained. Beans, *El Mercurio* proclaimed, had become "almost a luxury item."

A MIRACLE

During this period, on November 25, 1915, Augusto Pinochet was born in Valparaíso. He was the first child of Augusto Pinochet and Avelina Ugarte. The boy's father was a customs officer at the port, and the middle-class family felt the economic pinch when port revenues began to drop because of the Panama Canal and World War I. Even so, they lived in a large three-story house and had servants to help with housework and child care in a family that eventually grew to six children.

Every morning their nanny took the children out to play in a park across from the house. One day on the way home from the park, when Augusto was only four, he darted out into the street into the path of a horse-drawn cart. He was knocked to the ground and a wheel ran over his left knee. It did not seem serious at the time. The bruises and scrapes soon healed.

When Augusto was about to start school two years later, however, the knee swelled up painfully. Doctors diagnosed osteal

(bone) tuberculosis and recommended amputation of the leg as the only means of preventing the infection from spreading. His mother would not consent to the operation. Augusto also was anxious not to lose his leg. His dream was to become a soldier like his great uncle Alejandro Ugarte, who told him vivid stories of fighting in Peru. He knew he could not join the military with only one leg.

Augusto's mother, who had grown up in a convent boarding school, turned to prayer. She made a vow to the Virgin Mary that if her son got better, did not lose his leg, and entered military school, she would wear brown for fifteen years. Augusto would also wear brown, she promised, for ten years if a civilian and two if a soldier.

The answer to her prayers came in a newspaper announcement that a famous German surgeon was to visit Chile. She quickly secured an appointment. The traveling expert declared that the swelling was a benign hydroarthrosis (accumulation of fluid). He prescribed daily exposure to sunshine to heal the leg. Augusto spent that summer at

SAY IT EITHER WAY

Pinochet is pronounced both "Pee-noh-CHET," as though it were a Spanish name, and "Pee-noh-SHAY" as in the original French.

his grandparents' small farm with his siblings and cousins, sunbathing every day. The pain eased, and the swelling disappeared. For the rest of his life, Augusto considered the incident a miracle.

THE END OF THE REPUBLIC

In 1920 Arturo Alessandri ran for president on a platform promising social reforms to help Chile's poor and working classes. He won the election, but his Liberal Alliance (a coalition of centrist and Socialist parties) did not win control of Congress. The economic gap between rich and poor grew even wider, but Alessandri's reforms were blocked by the conservative majority.

In September 1924, the army stepped in to end the deadlock between the president and Congress. Intimidated by the military, Congress immediately passed the laws. Alessandri resigned and left the country. On September 11, a military junta made up of two generals and an admiral began to rule Chile.

The junta was only temporary. The three leaders soon selected a civilian to take over the presidency. A group of young officers, however, opposed the junta's choice. They staged a second coup a few months later. Setting up their own junta, they sent telegrams to

Alessandri begging him to return to complete his term as president of Chile. He eagerly resumed his office.

Alessandri's first priority was a new constitution. To write it, he created a large commission representing every political party, including the recently formed Communist Party of Chile. The military was also represented. Three and a half months later, the constitution was complete. Less than half the electorate turned out to vote in the plebiscite (a nationwide vote for or against a proposal), but 93 percent of them voted in favor of the constitution. It became law on Independence Day, September 18, 1925.

The new constitution shifted the balance of power between the president and the Congress back to the president, without the extensive powers of the 1833 constitution. The presidential term of office became six years instead of five, but immediate reelection was not permitted. For the first time in Chile's history, Catholicism was not the state religion. Church and state were declared separate. The constitution also gave workers the right to organize, promised concern for the social welfare of all citizens, and asserted the government's right to take private property for the public good.

A TIME OF TURMOIL

The constitution did not get a chance to prove its worth right away. By the time it was approved, Alessandri's interrupted term of office was over. His successor resigned after less than two years in office. Colonel Carlos Ibáñez del Campo, one of the young officers who had brought Alessandri back to Chile, became acting president. He secured his position by putting restrictions on the press, using informers to track down dissent, and banishing more than two hundred politicians to remote parts of Chile. Alessandri was exiled for calling Ibáñez a mule. The Communist Party was outlawed. Many of its leaders were sent to Isla Más Afuera, the most distant of the Juan Fernández Islands, located in the South Pacific Ocean about 400 miles (645 km) west of mainland Chile. Even some conservative politicians found themselves out of favor.

CARLOS IBÁÑEZ DEL CAMPO
took over the Chilean government in 1927 and ruled as a dictator.

In May 1927, Ibáñez held an election and declared himself a candidate. Only an exiled Communist leader dared to attempt to oppose him. Once officially installed as president, Ibáñez asked party leaders to agree among themselves on one slate of candidates for Congress. He then approved the list, and this slate became the congress for 1930 to 1934. No congressional elections were held. When opponents compared him to Benito Mussolini, the Fascist dictator who ruled Italy (from 1922 to 1943), Ibáñez proudly adopted the nickname "the Chilean Mussolini."

Ibáñez's dictatorship initiated a large program of building and repairing roads, bridges, railways, barracks, prisons, airfields, and port facilities. It also strengthened the military, creating Chile's first air force (which operated Chile's first airline), uniting all local police into one national police force (the carabineros), and purchasing weapons and ships for the army and the navy.

Chileans follow the Spanish custom of using two surnames. After a person's given name or names comes the father's family name, followed by the mother's family name. For example, the dictator's full name is Augusto Pinochet Ugarte. His oldest son is Augusto Pinochet Hiriart. Occasionally, the mother's family name is dropped or abbreviated. The matronymic (mother's family name) has been omitted in this book.

Ibáñez borrowed heavily from the United States to carry out his ambitious programs. But when the Chilean economy collapsed in 1930 in the worldwide Great Depression (1929–1941), his government could no longer pay interest on the loans. At the end of July 1931, Ibáñez fled the country, taking the train across the Andes to Argentina.

A well-liked member of the Radical Party, a center-left party that attracted middle-class voters, stepped into the presidency and was officially elected to complete Ibáñez's term of office. But his efforts to lead the country were undermined by conspiracies and plots. Supporters of Ibáñez and Alessandri kept trying to reinstate their heroes in public office. Taking advantage of the chaos, a trio of Socialists (one of them the commander of Chile's air force) seized the government for a brief twelve days in 1932 before the army stepped in to restore order. When elections were held in October 1932, Arturo Alessandri regained the presidency. Order was at last restored.

A DREAM COME TRUE

Growing up during this time of political turmoil, Augusto Pinochet attended private Catholic schools in Valparaíso and in Quillota, where the family had a country house. Augusto did not excel in school, barely squeaking by in most subjects. More to his liking were the fencing lessons he talked his father into letting him take. He also enjoyed boxing.

Augusto had his first taste of politics as a young teenager when he visited a conservative political club with school friends. They went for the free food, he wrote in his autobiography. When it turned out the organizers wanted the boys (who were too young to vote) to attend rallies and throw rocks and bottles, Augusto chose not to get involved. Politicians, he decided, were not to be trusted.

Augusto's father urged him to study medicine, but his mother encouraged his military dreams. Twice he applied to the Colégio Militar (military school) in Santiago and was turned down. He later claimed that the first rejection was owing to his young age and the second to his physical weakness. More likely, his poor grades hurt his chances most. On the third try, when he was seventeen, he was accepted. The morning in March 1933 when he enrolled in the school was "one of the happiest moments of my life."

He loved everything about the school—the uniforms, the schedules, the drills. He learned to present arms so well that only two months after entering the school, he was chosen to appear in an honor guard for President Alessandri's State of the Nation address in 1933. Wearing full dress uniform and a plumed helmet, he stood proudly at attention for the entire four hours of the speech.

He joined the Greco-Roman wrestling team and the sharpshooter team and was thrilled to see his name in the national paper *El Mercurio* for scoring sixty points against the University of Chile team in a shooting match. By the third year, even schoolwork began to appeal to him. The curriculum at last included real military subjects—military history, geopolitics, and military strategy.

Pinochet graduated as an ensign in the infantry at the end of December 1936. As a graduation present, his father gave him two brown suits, one light, one dark, so that he could honor his mother's vow when not in uniform. In gratitude for the miracle that had made his career possible, he placed a plaque in a local church. "Thank you, Mother mine," it read. "Succor [help] me always."

STARTING MILITARY LIFE

Pinochet enjoyed army life. He liked getting up early, the physical exercise, the rugged camp life, the camaraderie, and the practical jokes the men played on one another. He took great pride in carrying the flag in military parades and wearing his dress uniform to the opera. His friends teased him for being *"pomposo"* (pompous).

Like all military personnel, Pinochet moved around frequently. He was posted first to the infantry school in San Bernardo, only ten miles (16 km) south of Santiago, then to Concepción, and later to Valparaíso. In April 1940, by then a second lieutenant, he returned to the Infantry School, this time as a teacher.

That year Pinochet fell in love with Lucía Hiriart, a high school student who was several years younger than he was. His comrades called him *"infanticida"* (baby-killer), but Pinochet was determined to marry Lucía, which he did on January 30, 1943. Lucía was the daughter of Osvaldo Hiriart, a lawyer active in the Radical Party. Pinochet's new father-in-law was appointed minister of the interior in 1943.

During the Second World War, Chile at first remained neutral, as it had in World War I. Chile had long had good relations with Germany. Many Germans immigrated to Chile in the nineteenth century and settled among the lakes and mountains of the south. After the War of the Pacific, Chile had wanted to make its armies

THE UNITED STATES AND COMMUNISM IN LATIN AMERICA

After World War II ended in 1945, the United States became increasingly active in combating Communism in Latin America. The U.S. government provided military aid involving "the indoctrination, training and equipment of the armed forces of the other American republics." The Central Intelligence Agency (CIA) also played a major role in the effort. In 1954 the United States used the CIA to support and finance the ouster of a leftist government in Guatemala. After Fidel Castro brought Communist rule to Cuba, the CIA trained and supplied Cuban exiles to overthrow him. Their invasion of Cuba at the Bay of Pigs in 1961 failed. In 1965 U.S. troops invaded Santo Domingo (an island nation in the Caribbean Sea) to support a military dictatorship. The United States considered the regime an ally against Communism.

more professional. It invited military officers from Prussia, a part of Germany, to train Chilean troops. The gray uniforms and goose-step marching of the Chilean army date from this period.

Chile did declare war on Germany in 1942. Pinochet and his fellow officers followed the war, marking troop movements with colored thumbtacks on a map as news arrived from Europe. They especially admired the German general Erwin Rommel, whose tactics in North Africa earned him the nickname the Desert Fox. Pinochet later maintained that their interest in the German army was entirely a professional one. Politics, he said, bored him.

THE COLD WAR AFFECTS CHILE

After the war, Pinochet was posted to the mining town of Iquique. In 1946, while he was there, the Radical Party teamed up with the Communist Party to get their candidate Gabriel González elected president. The following year, however, the United States refused to extend credit to Chile as long as Communists participated in the government. González dismissed the three Communist ministers serving in his cabinet. When Communist workers went on strike in protest, the president declared a state of emergency.

That evening at nine o'clock, Pinochet received secret orders to immediately arrest Communist leaders in his region and escort them to a concentration camp in Pisagua, near Iquique. By dawn he had several hundred detainees at the camp.

Pinochet personally knew some of the arrested men, one of whom had helped him supply his troops when he was on maneuvers.

COLD WAR

The Cold War was a period of conflict, tension, and competition between the United States and the Soviet Union and their respective allies from 1945 to 1991. The two superpowers never fought each other directly. Instead, they engaged in propaganda and espionage; offered military, economic, and food aid to developing countries to win their support and to influence their internal politics; and built huge arsenals stocked with increasingly powerful nuclear warheads, missiles, and other up-to-the-minute technological inventions. These stockpiles assured both nations they had the capability to wipe each other off the face of the earth. For almost half a century, the Cold War dominated international relations and occasionally erupted into open warfare, as occurred in Korea (1950–1953), Vietnam (1957–1975), and Afghanistan (1979–1989).

He felt bad enough about the situation to invite them to dine with him in the officers' dining room.

While Pinochet was commander of the camp, a delegation of leftist congressmen came to inspect the camp. Among them was Senator Salvador Allende. Three decades later, Pinochet wrote that he refused the delegation permission to enter the camp. It is unlikely, however, that an army captain would have challenged visitors representing the government, and there is no other evidence that the inspectors were denied entry. It seems that Pinochet invented the story later to make it look like he had always been strongly anti-Communist. Whether the two men met at that time is unclear.

RISING THROUGH THE RANKS

Pinochet's best hope of military advancement was to gain admission to the War Academy in Santiago. With that goal in mind, he studied hard while he was in Iquique. Lucía Pinochet was so certain of his success that even before Pinochet took the entrance exam, she began selling the furniture so they could be ready to move right away.

Pinochet was in his element again at the War Academy. In his second and third years, in addition to taking classes there, he also began teaching courses at the military school, where he had started his training. He also edited a military magazine, *Cien Águilas* (100 Eagles).

Promoted to the rank of major after completing his studies at the War Academy, Pinochet spent a year commanding a regiment in Arica on the Peruvian border. In 1955 he returned to Santiago, to teach his favorite subjects at the War Academy—military geography and geopolitics.

Ambitious to add to his credentials, he also enrolled in the University of Chile to study law, finding time in the evenings to study and getting to classes as often as he could. But these studies were interrupted by a new assignment to teach at the War Academy in Quito, Ecuador. During his three and a half years there, Pinochet began writing books on geopolitics and other military subjects. Some became textbooks for military courses. Publishing these books helped Pinochet's advancement in the army.

In 1957 Pinochet made his first trip to the United States, with a group from the Ecuadorian academy. He visited the Pentagon in Washington, D.C., and traveled to New York City; El Paso, Fort Bliss, and Dallas, Texas; and Miami, Florida. The United States promoted these visits to encourage Latin American militaries to oppose Communism.

The year after he returned to Chile from Ecuador, Pinochet was promoted to lieutenant colonel and served in the northern city of Antofagasta for three years. He then returned to Santiago, this time as deputy director of the War Academy. He traveled twice more to the United States, in 1965 and 1968. Pinochet wrote later that he was impressed by the valor of U.S. troops fighting for democracy in Vietnam. By his third trip, he was a full colonel and celebrating his twenty-fifth wedding anniversary. His wife, Lucía, made the journey with him.

GAINS ON THE LEFT

During the years Pinochet was rising through the military ranks, Chile was once again stable. Elections took place without incident, and the military stayed out of politics. (Noncommissioned officers, enlisted men, and police were not even allowed to vote.) Many neighboring countries, meanwhile, suffered violent coups and rule by repressive military juntas or dictators.

Stability did not mean unanimity. Party politics continued to keep Chile immersed in partisanship. The pendulum swung from left to right and back again. For fourteen years, the Radical Party led Chile. Then Ibáñez regained the presidency—this time by a legal election—in 1952, and twelve years of right-wing rule followed.

Women were permitted to vote for the first time in 1949, and they gradually came to play a larger role in government. In 1958 parties of the left in Congress managed to rescind the *Ley Maldita* (cursed law) that had outlawed the Communist Party. They also succeeded in changing electoral laws to make it easier for citizens to register to vote. Ballots were made simpler and for the first time secret. Many of the new voters on the rolls were poor. Politics, once almost entirely controlled by the wealthy upper class, began to attract members of the middle and working classes.

Leftist parties gained followers, mainly because the poor still lacked adequate housing, health care, and access to education. Many impoverished families lived on the outskirts of Santiago and other cities in shacks made of old crates. Chileans called these shantytowns *callampas* (mushrooms) because they seemed to sprout overnight. These eyesores were a constant reminder of the inequities in Chilean society.

"[It was] painful [to see] ragged women with little kids in their arms begging for charity in the city center."

–José Roberto Rubio, Argentine visitor to Santiago in the 1960s

Pressure for change, coming from the working classes, attracted voters to the Socialist and Communist parties. It also helped the new Christian Democratic Party get a start. The Christian Democrats promised social reform through democracy—a "revolution in liberty," as the party slogan stated.

POLITICAL PARTIES

During the nineteenth century, Chile had developed a multi-party political system similar to those of many European countries. The parties represented the full political spectrum, including the liberal left, the center, and the conservative right.

In the early twentieth century, Chile's four principal parties were the Conservatives, the Liberals, the Radicals, and the Democrats. Smaller parties existed both to the right and the left of these groups. In 1933 several smaller leftist groups joined to create the Socialist Party. About that same time, rightists founded a National Socialist Party (inspired by the Hitler-led German Nazi Party) and the National Falange (formed by Conservative Christians interested in social reform).

The National Falange later merged with another splinter group from the Conservative Party. Together they formed the Christian Democrat Party in 1957, which quickly won a wide following.

Parties often joined forces to gain representation. By forming a coalition and backing one candidate for president or a slate of candidates for congressional or municipal elections, even smaller groups could hope to gain a voice in government.

By 1964, as presidential elections approached in Chile, the United States became concerned about the possible results of this broader electorate in Chile. Especially worrisome to the United States was a coalition of Democrats, Socialists, and Communists known as FRAP (Frente de Acción Popular, or Front for Popular Action). Its platform included nationalizing large businesses and banks, redistributing farmland, and lowering the voting age to eighteen. FRAP's candidate was Senator Salvador Allende. The 1964 election was his third attempt to win the presidency, an office he had come close to winning in 1958.

The U.S. Central Intelligence Agency (CIA), feared that a FRAP victory would mean losing a battle in the Cold War between the United States and the Soviet Union, by now comprised of fourteen other republics besides Russia. It poured $2.6 million into the campaign of Allende's strongest opponent, Eduardo Frei, the Christian Democratic candidate. The Vatican and Christian Democratic parties in several Western European countries also contributed to Frei's race. In a strongly negative campaign, the Christian Democrats implied that Allende would make Chile a satellite of the Soviet Union.

Allende won 38.9 percent of the vote in the three-way race. Frei, however, won with an astounding 56.1 percent. The candidate for the right won only 5 percent of the vote. The extremely imbalanced outcome probably occurred because right-wing voters ditched their own weak candidate and cast their votes to stop Allende. But Frei's election set Chile on a course that would pit rich against poor and right against left.

EDUARDO FREI RAN FOR PRESIDENT of Chile without success in 1958. The United States backed his candidacy in 1964, and he won the election.

CHAPTER 2

WHEN PINOCHET RETURNED FROM THE UNITED STATES IN 1968,
he was annoyed that a classmate from military school had been appointed director of the War Academy. He did not wish to be sub-director to a director who graduated the same year he did. He even thought of retiring from the army rather than work at the academy.

Pinochet did not complain, but he pointed the fact out to his superiors. At first, nothing changed, but later, he was offered a staff post with the general in command of the Second Division of the army. Then news came that he had been selected to attend a course to prepare him for high command. By the end of the year, Pinochet received news that he would be promoted to brigadier general. He was deeply moved, he wrote later, at having reached this pinnacle of a military career, one of his greatest aspirations.

That year Pinochet's classmate was removed from the director-

ship of the war academy. Some of the officers at the academy protested against army cutbacks, and the army commanders thought the director had put them up to it. When this happened, Pinochet was grateful he had not been named director. Had he held that office, he reasoned, he might have lost his chance for promotion to general. Incidents like this fed Pinochet's tendency to consider himself destined for leadership.

As he rose through the ranks, Pinochet had carefully avoided becoming involved in politics. Even his marriage to a politician's daughter did not soften his views of political life. When he became brigadier general and took command of the Sixth Division in Iquique, however, he also received his first political assignment. President Frei appointed him acting governor of the region of Tarapacá, of which Iquique is the capital.

For the first time, Pinochet had civilian as well as military duties. "Destiny was once again generous in the preparation of my future," Pinochet wrote later. His civilian work, he said, gave him practical and precise knowledge of social, political, and economic affairs of government. But his military attitude did not help him in civilian matters.

In August 1969, the students of a technical college in Iquique staged a sit-in, or nonviolent occupation, at the school to protest a lack of instructional materials. As acting governor, Pinochet had to deal with the problem. At first Pinochet asked the students' parents to tell the students to go home. This approach failed because the parents agreed with the students that the school needed more supplies. In response, Pinochet ordered that water, electricity, and phone service to the school be cut off. He then surrounded the school with police and ordered them to arrest any student who tried to leave.

Appalled at Pinochet's actions, the government in Santiago intervened and ordered Pinochet to release the students. The ministry of education agreed to meet the students' requests for more resources for their school. Pinochet followed the orders, but he wrote later that he felt that by not enforcing discipline, President Frei was losing all authority.

TRYING TO STOP ALLENDE

The Frei administration was having problems. In spite of massive U.S. support—economic aid, military assistance, and covert CIA propaganda against leftist FRAP candidates—the Christian Democratic Party was being battered both by opposition from a reunited right and internal differences with its own more liberal members. As Frei's six-year term came to an end, some Christian Democrats, concerned that their party had accomplished too little for the poor, bolted from the party. They joined a new leftist coalition called Popular Unity (Unidad Popular, or UP). Its candidate was Salvador Allende, running on a platform promising a peaceful, democratic "Chilean road to socialism."

On election day, September 4, 1970, Allende won 36.4 percent of the popular vote, well ahead of the two other candidates. Since he received a plurality (less than half of the votes cast but more than the other candidates), not a majority, the Chilean Congress had to confirm the vote on October 24. In the past, Congress had always supported the candidate with the most votes.

In the United States, President Richard M. Nixon and his national security adviser Henry Kissinger were determined to stop Allende from assuming the presidency. Some right-wing Chileans, among them a number of military officers, agreed. The anti-Soviet propaganda encouraged and funded by the United States had persuaded many Chileans that Allende was part of an international conspiracy to establish a totalitarian government. They felt he was not a strong believer

SALVADOR ALLENDE WON MORE votes than the opposition in the 1970 election but didn't receive a majority of all the votes cast.

in constitutional democracy, although he really was. During the campaign, one anti-Allende poster showed a Soviet tank parked by the presidential residence, La Moneda.

The CIA used two different tactics to try to stop Allende. One was to bribe members of Congress to vote for the runner-up (who won 34.9 percent of the vote), seventy-four-year-old former president Arturo Alessandri, candidate of the new right-wing National Party. The other was to supply weapons and tactical advice to

U.S. EFFORTS TO TOPPLE ALLENDE

When U.S. efforts to prevent the Chilean Congress from ratifying Allende's election as president failed, President Nixon swore that he would bring about Allende's downfall by making "the [Chilean] economy scream." The United States took a number of steps against the Allende administration, both openly and covertly.

Hoping to create a severe economic crisis in Chile, all U.S. funding—except military—was cut off. The United States also put pressure on the World Bank (an international financial organization) to make no loans to Chile and pressured U.S. corporations to make no investments there.

"With regard to the *Chilean military*," Henry Kissinger, the national security adviser, wrote to Nixon in a memorandum, "we are maintaining our military mission on a 'business as usual' basis in order to maintain maximum contacts with the Chilean military." Military support, in fact, increased. Sales of U.S. military equipment to Chile during Allende's three years in office were triple what they were the three years before that. Training and other military aid also rose sharply.

military officers considering a coup. These conspirators planned to provoke the army into action by kidnapping the commander in chief of the army, General René Schneider. The plot went seriously awry. Schneider was fatally wounded in the attempt to abduct him. As Schneider lay dying in the hospital, the Congress voted 153 to 35 to confirm Allende's presidency. Even right-wing politicians denounced Schneider's death, the first political assassination in Chile since that of Diego Portales in 1837.

Other U.S. actions were covert. Between the murder of General Schneider in 1970 and Allende's overthrow in 1973, a secret national security organization known as the Forty Committee funded CIA operations in Chile with eight million dollars. This money supported strikes (such as the miners' strikes and the truckers' strikes), which were aimed at hurting Chile's economy; the right-wing radio station, Radio Agricultura, which conducted a smear campaign against Allende; the women who organized right-wing protests; and the Patria y Libertad (Fatherland and Freedom) illegal militia (citizen army). Some of the money also went to legitimate political parties, such as the Democratic Confederation. They hoped to gain enough support in the congressional elections of March 1973 to impeach Allende. Opposition newspapers, such as *El Mercurio*, also received CIA donations and published propaganda articles written by the CIA or editors and journalists on the CIA payroll.

The goal of all these tactics was to encourage opposition to Allende within Chile. In fact, Allende gained support during the three years he was in office. The actions of the United States did, however, contribute to the chaos and unrest and helped widen the divisions in Chilean society.

NEAR THE TOP OF THE LADDER

When Salvador Allende was elected in September 1970, Pinochet probably did not make the sharply anti-Communist speech he included in the book he wrote nine years later. Still, he was likely upset to see the leftist coalition win the presidency. His military training had made him mistrustful of all politicians, especially those of the left. But he was also saddened by the death of General Schneider, whom he admired, and he kept well apart from right-wing conspiracies. Unlike another general, Roberto Viaux, who had supported Schneider's abduction, Pinochet did not think army officers had the right to protest. He admired military discipline and order. For him, obedience to his superiors was both an ingrained habit and a core belief.

In 1971 Pinochet was promoted to major general and given command of the Santiago garrison. He was in the capital and was a daily witness to the activities of the Allende administration. It was making good on its promise to put Chile on the road to Socialism. New laws provided education, work, and health care for the poor, raised the minimum wage, nationalized the large copper mines, and broke up large estates into cooperative farms owned and run by agricultural workers.

"Nacionalizando el cobre / dejaremos de ser probres."
"By nationalizing copper / We shall cease to be poor."
—Chilean Communist Party slogan, 1970[25]

PRESIDENT ALLENDE *(RIGHT)* **WELCOMES CUBAN LEADER FIDEL CASTRO**
(left) **at the Santiago airport in 1971. In 1964 Chile had joined other North and South American countries in refusing economic and political ties with Cuba.**

After a successful first year, however, Allende's program began to falter. The price of copper on the international market dropped, leaving the government without funds for its social programs. Prices for consumer goods rose, and there were shortages, particularly of food and everyday necessities.

As the commander of army troops stationed in the city, Pinochet was responsible for maintaining security and order. When Fidel Castro, the Marxist leader of Cuba, visited Chile in November 1971, Pinochet personally escorted him on several ceremonial occasions.

Shortly before Castro left, a right-wing women's group organized a protest they called the March of the Empty Pots. Banging pots and pans together, several thousand women marched through the streets of Santiago to call attention to food shortages. Alongside them were men with clubs to protect them. A riot broke out between the protesters and supporters of Allende. Carabineros dispersed the crowds with tear gas, and Pinochet declared a curfew.

In January 1972, Pinochet was appointed head of the joint chiefs of staff of the army. He became second in command after General Carlos Prats, who had replaced Schneider as commander in chief.

That year saw a steady worsening of conditions in Chile. Poor weather brought lower harvests. Prices kept rising rapidly. When the government tried to control the prices, people resorted to buying and selling goods illegally. In October, when plans were announced to form a government-owned company to transport freight, Chile's truckers went on strike. More than twenty-three thousand trucks were idled. Shops and small businesses closed.

A POLICE OFFICER TRIES TO RESTRAIN A PROTESTER AT A DEMONSTRATION in Santiago. Hundreds of people staged the demonstration in 1972 to show their support for striking truckers.

To deal with the problem, Allende asked three top military officers to serve in his cabinet. General Prats became minister of the interior. While Prats negotiated an end to the truckers' strike, Pinochet became the acting commander of the army.

ALLENDE'S CHALLENGE

In March 1973, Allende's government faced an important test—congressional elections. The principal opposition parties, the National Party and the Christian Democratic Party, joined forces. They hoped to gain a two-thirds majority, allowing them to impeach Allende. Allende's UP wanted to win a majority to make it easier to pass laws supporting their Socialist platform. When the results came in, both sides claimed victory, but neither attained its goal. The UP had increased its representation to 43.4 percent of the vote. The opposition still had a majority, 55 percent, but not one large enough to unseat Allende.

The UP nevertheless continued to press for new reforms, among them a national curriculum for Chile's schools. Many parents and church leaders denounced the planned curriculum for not teaching religion and family values. The National Party described it as "thought control." The military members of Allende's cabinet resigned in protest of the curriculum.

A worse problem was the increasing violence. The more militant members of the UP had no patience for congressional debates and voting. Trained in Marxist-Leninist thinking, they believed only an armed revolution could bring about an egalitarian society. They organized workers and seized farms and factories illegally and without compensation to the owners. In retaliation, right-wing extremists formed illegal militias that disrupted political rallies and bombed bridges, railways, and government offices. One of these right-wing groups, known as Patria y Libertad (Fatherland and Freedom), was financed by the CIA. To disarm these groups, the Chilean Congress outlawed private ownership of automatic weapons and passed a law allowing the military to conduct weapons searches.

The military, meanwhile, became the target of both the left and the right. Militant Socialists tried to get enlisted men to mutiny against their officers. Right-wing agitators taunted the armed forces for not taking control of the government.

On June 29, 1973, a tank regiment attacked La Moneda. Instigated by the right-wing militia Patria y Libertad, the one hundred soldiers in the regiment hoped other army units would be inspired to join them. Instead, armed units led by generals Prats and Pinochet quickly put down the coup attempt.

The *tancazo* (as the tank attack was called) failed miserably, but other plots were hatching. Pinochet later wrote that he began planning the September 11 coup more than a year before it occurred. However, there is no other evidence that he was directly involved until a few days before. Other army officers, working with naval and air force officers, took the initiative and organized a well-coordinated attack.

On August 21, the wives of some army officers staged a noisy demonstration in front of Prats's home. They shouted insults and demanded Prats's resignation. Scattering dried corn on the ground, they accused him of being too chicken to lead a coup.

The next day, after meeting with his top officers, General Prats resigned, saying he could no longer command an army that had

WOMEN WAVE WHITE HANDKERCHIEFS AT AN ANTI-MARXIST PROTEST IN Santiago in 1973. The protesters demanded Allende's resignation.

lost confidence in him. Allende named Pinochet to succeed Prats as commander in chief. Prats had no doubt at all that Pinochet was fully committed to defending the Chilean government. "President," he had heard Pinochet say to Allende, "be aware that I am ready to lay down my life in defense of the constitutional government that you represent."

It may be that Pinochet was hedging his bets. He had worked long enough for the highest levels of government to know all their plans. He also kept an eye on the generals. He was qualified, well informed, and in the perfect position to organize a coup. But he had no intention of risking a tancazo. Known for his skills at poker, Pinochet was not about to show his hand.

The U.S. ambassador to Chile at the time tells the story that a U.S. Intelligence officer said to Pinochet earlier that year, "You are on a sinking ship. When are you going to act?" Pinochet reportedly replied, "Not until our legs get wet. If we act too soon, the people from all sides would unite against us."

There was also another reason for waiting. Up until the end of August, Pinochet had Prats to consider. Conspiring against Allende at that time would have meant engaging in mutiny against his superior officer. He had spent the last forty years following orders, ever since proudly entering military school. That's what being a soldier meant—obeying orders without questions.

Once Prats had resigned, Pinochet arrived at the top of the hierarchy. He was in charge of the army. The orders were up to him. If he joined the coup, he could take the army with him. Even well into September, however, Pinochet did not seem to have fully made up his mind what to do. He had taken an oath to defend Allende and the constitution of Chile, and he believed in vows.

THE COUP PACT

On September 8, Brigadier General Sergio Arellano Stark reportedly visited Pinochet at home and informed him that a coup would be carried out on September 11. A group of army generals supported the coup, as did Vice Admiral José Toribio Merino, the second-highest ranking commander of the navy, and General Gustavo Leigh, the head of the air force. He gave Pinochet the choice of resigning and stepping aside (as Prats had done) or joining the coup as head of the army. Pinochet did not give a direct answer. He only slammed his fist on the table and said, "I am not a Marxist!"

The next day, Pinochet met with Allende. He said nothing about Arellano's visit and what he had learned about the planned coup.

Instead, he assured the president that the army was prepared to deal with any conspiracies.

Pinochet spent that evening relaxing at home with his family and a few family friends. They were celebrating the fourteenth birthday of his youngest daughter, Jacqueline. General Leigh interrupted the festivities. He took Pinochet aside to discuss the urgency of the coup. He wanted to be sure that Pinochet was with the plotters. Then two naval officers arrived with a message from Admiral Merino. Merino asked for their signatures on a paper giving the date and hour of the coup. Leigh did not hesitate. Pinochet seemed less certain. He looked around for his official seal.

Pinochet's apparent hesitation may have been caused by a difference of opinion about the date: Pinochet wrote later he favored September 14 for the coup. It would give them more time to prepare, and no one would be suspicious about troop movements as it was the day when the army would be rehearsing for their annual military day parade on September 19.

Or Pinochet may have been still deciding what to do. Any number of questions could have been whirling through his mind. How much did he trust these men? How could he betray his oath and the president who trusted him so completely? Was he willing to give up his career and possibly his life for a Marxist? How many of his officers would remain loyal to Chile's constitution, and how many would obey their commander in chief no matter what he ordered them to do? If he agreed, was thirty-six hours enough to mobilize the army?

He found the seal. "Agreed, A. Pinochet," he wrote, then added the commander in chief stamp to the handwritten pact. He bid the men good night and rejoined the family party, all smiles and apologies, the gracious host. He said nothing, even to his wife, about what lay ahead.

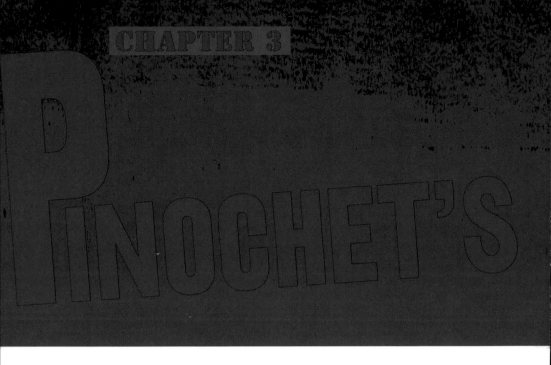

CHAPTER 3

PINOCHET'S

PINOCHET'S RELAXED MANNER FOOLED HIS FAMILY AND GUESTS,
but he did not sleep well that night or the night after that. Monday,
September 10, was spent pretending everything was fine while
hammering out details of the coup at private meetings held in the
ministry of defense. A proclamation stating the purpose of the coup
had to be agreed on and General César Mendoza of the carabineros brought into the plot.

Already a rivalry was developing between Leigh and Pinochet
for leadership. As they prepared a proclamation to be broadcast
the next day, Leigh pointed out that he should preside over the
planned junta since, according to military rules, he had seniority
over Pinochet. Allende had appointed him commanding general
of the air force on August 20. Pinochet's appointment came three
days later. But the army has seniority over the air force, Pinochet

THE FOUR LEADERS OF THE 1973 COUP SALUTE DURING INDEPENDENCE DAY celebrations in Santiago. From left, they are Gustavo Leigh, Augusto Pinochet, José Toribio Merino, and César Mendoza.

responded, because it has existed far longer than the air force. Pinochet therefore became the president of the junta, although he had only joined the coup organized by Leigh and Merino at the last moment.

On Monday night, the Chilean fleet sailed out of Valparaíso to join U.S. naval ships for annual joint exercises at sea. UP leaders breathed a sigh of relief. Many naval officers were suspected of plotting to overthrow the government. With the navy out at sea, President Allende would not have to worry about a coup for a few more days.

That night the president worked on a speech to be delivered the next day. He planned to propose a plebiscite allowing Chileans to vote directly, yes or no, as to whether they wanted new elections. It was his final solution to all the problems that had been closing in on him. He was ready to resign if that is what the majority of the Chilean people wanted.

The fleet's departure, however, was part of the conspirators' plan. At midnight, the fleet turned around and returned to the bay of Valparaíso to provide support for naval ground troops in capturing the city at 6 A.M. on Tuesday, September 11. The capture of the port was so swift and easy that the ships were not even needed, although their sudden, very visible return may have helped prevent any opposition.

Army troops simultaneously captured Concepción. Taken completely by surprise, citizens there attempted no resistance to the armed soldiers.

Meanwhile, military units knocked on the doors of leftist radio stations across the country saying they had orders to search for weapons. Used to such harassment, station operators let them in. The soldiers then smashed and disabled all broadcasting equipment. The military also took control over all public utilities, such as electricity and water.

Pinochet was up early. He did his usual morning exercises before putting on his combat uniform. On his way to work, he stopped to see his sleeping grandchildren at his son Augusto's house. He had already sent his wife Lucía and his two younger children to an army base in the Andes. The base commander was loyal to Allende. They would be safe if the coup failed.

He then headed to the Army Communications Center on the outskirts of Santiago, post one in the military plans of the coup plotters. Post two was at the War Academy, where General Leigh was directing the Chilean Air Force. Post three, at the military school, was manned by the radio operators who engineered the communications links among the coup leaders and who secretly recorded the conversations that took place that day. General Mendoza was stationed at post four, and Vice Admiral Patricio Carvajal represented the naval forces at post five in the ministry of defense.

President Allende received an early morning telephone call from a carabinero officer who had been notified of the coup by one of his men in Valparaíso. Allende immediately called Pinochet's house, only to be told that the general would call him back. By 7:30 Allende was on his way to La Moneda, still unaware of the extent of the plot to unseat him. His two grown daughters came with him.

The attack on La Moneda began about nine and lasted several hours. Allende refused to resign. He also turned down offers of a plane to take him into exile. By then he knew that Pinochet, the general he had completely trusted, had turned against him. Perhaps he realized that a person that devious would be unlikely to allow him to live. Like President Balmaceda in 1891, he chose to take his own life. First, he addressed the Chilean people over Radio Magallanes, which had a mobile unit that had managed to evade destruction by the military. Then he persuaded his daughters and his cabinet members and other supporters to leave the palace. Alone, in a velvet-draped reception room lined with the portraits of Chile's presidents, he shot himself with a gun that Fidel Castro gave him when Castro visited Chile.

EXCERPTS FROM ALLENDE'S LAST SPEECH

About 10:00 A.M. on September 11, as tanks shelled La Moneda and snipers fired back, Salvador Allende made a final speech over the only radio station loyal to his government still on the air. He thanked his followers for their loyalty and urged them to carry on but not sacrifice themselves.

"This will probably be the last opportunity I have to address you. . . . But my words are not spoken in bitterness, rather, in disappointment.

"Let there be a moral judgment on those who have betrayed the oath they took as Chilean soldiers and commanders-in-chief. . . .

"In the face of these events, all that remains for me to say to the workers is, 'I shall not surrender.' Placed in a crucial moment of our history, I will pay with my life for the loyalty of my people. . . . They are strong, they are able to subdue us, but social processes cannot be detained by either crime or force. History is on our side, and it is made by the people. . . .

"In these final hours before my voice is silenced, I want to make one point. It was the united reactionary forces of foreign capital and imperialism that created the climate for the army to break their tradition. . . .

"Radio Magallanes will surely soon be silenced, and the calm tone of my voice will no longer reach you. It does not matter. You shall continue to hear it. I shall always be with you, and you will remember me as a dignified man who was loyal to his country."

"The people must defend themselves, but not sacrifice themselves. The people shall not let themselves be destroyed nor demolished, but they shall not let themselves be humiliated either."

"Long live Chile! Long live the people! Long live the workers! These are my last words. I am convinced my sacrifice shall not be in vain. I am convinced that, at least, it shall serve as a moral judgment on the felony, cowardice and treason that lay waste our land."

In storming the palace, the army met some resistance from pro-UP militants firing from the roofs and upper floors of buildings around La Moneda. Allende's bodyguards shot at the attackers. But Allende's supporters lacked sufficient weapons and organization to mount a successful defense.

In a few places around the country, workers attempted to fight back. Several skirmishes would take place over the next few days. By nightfall on September 11, however, virtually all of Chile was in the hands of the military forces.

THE JUNTA SPEAKS

The four coup leaders appeared on television that night. Pinochet spoke first, bluntly, without smiling, in the staccato voice of someone giving orders. He did not make a long speech. One sentence about "patriotic duty" to save the country from "chaos" explained his actions. He then announced that a complete turnover in the government would take place: a new cabinet (to be made up entirely of military officers), new governors, and new civil servants. Diplomatic relations with foreign countries would continue as before, he said, with the exception of Cuba and others to be studied. The junta would oversee all branches of government. "Congress will be in recess until further notice."

The other officers each spoke in turn. General Leigh took a more elegant and scholarly tone, explaining the coup as a "sad and painful mission" but insisting that the "Marxist cancer" that brought "economic, moral, and social disaster" to Chile could no longer be tolerated. Vice Admiral Merino played the "we-did-not-want-to-do-this" card. We would much prefer to be out at sea in our boats, he said. But patriotism called. General Mendoza said that the coup was not a matter of crushing an ideology or of personal vengeance but of reestablishing public order and returning the country to the way of the constitution and the laws of the republic.

As the speeches ended, the people watching the broadcast must have reacted with mixed emotions. For supporters of Allende, the scariest speech was the first one. The others stirred more hope, especially the last one: the coup was not a matter of vengeance, not a question of stamping out Marxism, but a step toward returning to constitutional government.

It had been a frightening day for all Chileans. The president was dead, La Moneda had been bombed and burned, the center of town was left pockmarked with bullets, and uniformed men with machine guns were enforcing a curfew. But most Chileans thought things would soon sort themselves out. This shocking event would end, and Chile would have elections and a new government. While leftists mourned Allende's death, many rightists hung out Chilean flags and popped open bottles of champagne.

PINOCHET TAKES THE LEAD

Although Pinochet joined the coup at the last moment, his role was of the utmost importance for its success. He held the top position in the largest branch of the armed forces. He had a record of long, loyal service, unlike some of the other army coup plotters who had earlier engaged in protests or failed attempts to interfere in politics. Many officers knew him as their professor at the military school or the War

Academy. He was probably someone they trusted to act reasonably in a crisis. Leigh and Merino knew that without Pinochet's support, the army might split apart, with some soldiers joining the coup and others protecting the government. With Pinochet's leadership, on the other hand, the army was more likely to hold together.

But neither Leigh nor Merino expected Pinochet to seize control of the government. The junta was, in their view, to be a joint rule. The four members would work together to restore order. According to the first decree they issued on September 11, the junta, not any one member of it, was assuming "Supreme Command of the Nation." When the junta held press conferences, their aides-de-camp had to find sites with doors wide enough that the members could walk in four abreast.

Shortly after the coup, Pinochet explained the idea to the press. "The junta works as a single entity," he said. "I was elected president [of the junta] because I am the oldest. . . . But I will not be the only president of the junta; after a while, Admiral Merino will be, then General Leigh, and so on. I am not an ambitious man; I would not want to seem to be a usurper of power." Events would prove this was not entirely true.

MILITARY CONTROL

Pinochet soon established supremacy over the other junta members. His authority came from more than just his title. From the start, the junta assigned military men to govern at every level. Chile was divided into thirteen regions, and each was assigned a military administrator (called an *intendente*). Almost all of Chile's fifty-one provinces were assigned military governors. Military mayors took over every city and town. Military officers also became heads of industries that had been nationalized by the two previous presidents of Chile and managers of state-owned factories and farms.

Even the universities were militarized. The commander of a parachute regiment was appointed head of the University of Chile in Santiago. He arrived in military style, wearing his full uniform as he dropped down onto the campus by parachute. Military investigators determined which faculty members would be allowed to retain their teaching positions. Those suspected of leftist political sympathies were arrested, exiled, or fired. Students, too, faced investigations and arrests. Many were expelled or had their scholarships canceled.

"[I saw] them throwing books and papers out the windows, and bringing them down by the elevator load from the building, just shoveling them out, shoveling them onto a fire. . . . The officers and men were proudly standing around the fire while they kept shoveling more books on, watching it burn with big smiles on their faces."

—Jim Ritter, American professor at the Catholic University in Santiago, describing what he saw during his arrest (for an expired visa), September 23, 1973

Pinochet depended on the unquestioning discipline that members of the military and the police were trained to observe. To fill all the government positions formerly held by civilians, Pinochet called on many retired generals. He also expanded the armed forces. The number of military troops in Chile rose from sixty thousand in 1973 to eighty-eight thousand in 1980. The army grew most, increasing in size by two-thirds.

Initially the junta members assigned themselves to different areas. The navy looked to economic matters, the air force to the social sector, and the police to agriculture, while the army dealt with political administration. Within a few years, however, Pinochet was involved in every sector. The army was the largest of the military services, and the majority of government positions went to army personnel. This helped Pinochet maintain his supremacy over the other junta members.

THE CARAVAN OF DEATH

The coup itself had been quickly won, and the number of casualties on September 11 itself was not high. But Pinochet, Leigh, and Merino were intent on abolishing Marxism, which they argued threatened the Chilean way of life. In their view, Marxists were internal enemies of the state, and they planned to wage war on them.

Immediately after the coup, the junta published lists of people it wished to question. Many of these people came to government offices of their own free will. They had committed no crimes and felt confident that the junta would not charge them with anything they had not done. Their trust was quickly shattered.

Tens of thousands of people were arrested and detained. Most were Chilean citizens, but many were foreign visitors. Some of these were refugees from dictatorships in neighboring countries. When the police ran out of space in the jails, barracks, police stations, warships, and various other facilities, they herded about seven thousand people into the soccer stadium in Santiago. Detention camps were set up all over Chile, from Pisagua in the north to Dawson Island in the Strait of Magellan. Some of those arrested were released after days or weeks of detention, but many were tortured and killed, sometimes without even a hasty military trial. Thousands were banished from Chile, forced to leave immediately

HASTILY CONSTRUCTED WALLS AND TOWERS SURROUND THE PUCHUNCAVI
detention center near Valparaíso. It was once a popular beach resort.

> *"We became confused over how long we were there. We couldn't tell night from day. We don't know if it was seven, eight, or nine days. It was a loss of human dignity to be stripped, and many sailors were laughing at us."*
>
> —Maria Huerta, twenty-year-old student, who was detained and tortured on a Chilean naval ship in September 1973

with only the clothes on their backs. Their abandoned homes and possessions were looted or destroyed.

In early October, Pinochet sent General Sergio Arellano, who had led and organized the army officers in planning the coup, to visit five military bases. His mission was "to inspect the system of military justice," or to make certain that Allende supporters were being just as ruthlessly arrested and executed elsewhere as in Santiago. As a result, seventy-two people were murdered by military firing squads. Arellano's two-week tour came to be known as the Caravan of Death.

THE PRESIDENT UNELECTED

Pinochet, however, never gave up his place as president of the junta and was soon pushing the others into electing him president of Chile. On June 17, 1974, he presented his three colleagues with a decree giving him the title supreme chief of the nation (which perhaps intentionally resembled the supreme director title of Chile's first president, Bernardo O'Higgins). It will make the government more efficient, he argued. After some discussion, they gave in.

Ten days later, when the decree was to be made public, the three junta members discovered that Pinochet had planned a formal inauguration, complete with a new

PINOCHET SPEAKS AT A NEWS conference in Paraguay in May 1974.

presidential sash. The old one had burned in the coup. Leigh was the angriest. "You think you're God," he yelled at Pinochet.

"I'm not going to allow the country to be played around with," Pinochet shouted back and banged his fist down so hard on a table that its glass top cracked.

At the ceremony itself, he was the picture of humility. After the Supreme Court justice had placed the sash over Pinochet's shoulders, Pinochet gave a short speech thanking the judge for an honor he had "never imagined, much less sought."

Pinochet promptly expanded his offices. He took two floors in the modern high-rise building where the government was housed while La Moneda was being repaired. The other junta members were each assigned one floor of the same building, all below the offices of the supreme chief of the nation. In December of that year, Pinochet changed his title to simply president of Chile. It was a clever move. It made him sound less like a dictator and more like someone who had been elected to office.

MILITARY INTELLIGENCE

By November 1973, Pinochet had formed the National Intelligence Directorate, known as the DINA. Most of the agents recruited to work for the DINA came from the military. Some were sent to train with the military in Brazil and in South Africa. By 1977 there were several thousand of these secret police. Their main targets were members of the Communist Party and especially MIR, a leftist revolutionary organization.

Torture was widely used. "The members of the MIR *must* be tortured," Pinochet said. "Without torture they don't sing." A concentration camp at Tejas Verdes in San Antonio, 58 miles (93 km) west of Santiago, and the Villa Grimaldi, a mansion in a residential neighborhood of Santiago, became especially notorious for the savage cruelty of the interrogation techniques used there. They were inflicted on men and women, young and old alike.

Some victims of torture were later released, but many victims of DINA operations were arrested and never heard from again. They simply disappeared. Families often did not know whether loved ones arrested by the DINA agents were alive or dead. Only years later did information come to light of DINA massacres, burials in remote areas, and dumping of bodies in the Pacific Ocean.

Not all DINA operations were directed against Marxists. Members of any left-leaning party, union organizers, people who went out after curfew or criticized the regime risked arrest. Men with long hair and even couples kissing in public were similarly harassed. DINA agents hauled away one young man for not standing up when the national anthem was played at a Santiago night club. He was later released, but only after a night of harsh questioning.

The DINA was also useful to Pinochet when he wanted to eliminate critics and rivals within the military. Several senior officers who had been loyal to Allende or who questioned Pinochet's tactics died in mysterious circumstances.

Pinochet allowed the DINA to operate outside Chile as well. General Prats and his wife, who were exiled to Argentina by Pinochet, were assassinated by a car bomb in Buenos Aires, the Argentine capital, a year after the coup. A former Christian

DESAPARECIDOS— THE DISAPPEARED

Victims who vanish during a military dictatorship are said to have been "disappeared." Often arrested in the middle of the night, these victims are taken to secret places of detention, tortured for information, executed, and disposed of. All records of their arrest and detention—and sometimes even of their existence—are destroyed or kept secret.

Democratic leader and his wife were badly injured in another DINA attack in Rome, Italy, in 1975. A year later, another car bomb, this time in Washington, D.C., killed Orlando Letelier, a Chilean exile who had served in President Allende's cabinet, and Ronni Moffitt, a young American woman working for him. International criticism finally led Pinochet to dismantle the DINA in 1977, but he immediately replaced it with a smaller, army-based intelligence arm, the National Intelligence Center, or CNI, which carried on with espionage and assassinations.

SIDELINING RIVALS

Pinochet was careful to sideline any competition. Not every rival was purged by assassination, though. As both commander in chief of the army and head of government, he could easily change an officer's assignment. Generals who gained popular support in a government post were quickly reassigned back to their units.

Most military assignments in the government were of short duration, only one or two years. Officers were usually glad to get back to army life, because promotions came from army service, not government work. For Pinochet, regular rotations of duty were a simple way of preventing any military officer from becoming too involved in government policy.

Pinochet could also remove rivals by forcing them to retire. Early on, the junta members had granted themselves indefinite terms of office. This gave them full control over the careers of those beneath them. They could promote officers who were loyal and helpful and retire those they suspected of disagreeing with their policies.

Of the other junta members, General Leigh was the most constant source of friction for Pinochet. From the start, Leigh considered himself, not Pinochet, the leader and the organizer of the coup, and he often acted independently of Pinochet. In 1978 Leigh gave a speech at the aviation school emphasizing the need for Chile to return to democracy. When he later repeated his support for more democracy in an interview with an Italian newspaper, Pinochet expelled Leigh from the junta and replaced him with a more pliant air force general.

With Leigh out of the picture, Pinochet felt assured enough to publish a book rewriting the story of the 1973 coup to give himself a more central role than he had actually played. He called it *El día decisivo* (The Crucial Day). Written as an interview with questions and answers (no interviewer or ghost writer is identified), the book suggests he masterminded the coup and portrays him as a hero for liberating Chile from becoming a pro-Soviet totalitarian state.

By the end of the 1970s, Pinochet had control over the entire government of Chile. The junta still existed, but Pinochet had the last word. "Not a leaf moves in Chile if I don't move it," he said to journalists in 1981. "Let that be clear."

ECONOMIC CHANGES

Pinochet knew that economic changes were needed to bolster support of his regime. The upper classes wanted lower taxes and the return of properties taken during the Frei and Allende years. In a complete reversal of Allende's programs, Pinochet's ministers of finance and economy removed price controls on staple products, cut back on public spending, and returned a number of state-owned businesses to private hands.

These policies did not immediately improve Chile's economy, partly because of problems outside of Chile. The price of copper on world markets dropped in the mid-1970s, and the price of oil rose steeply. Prices in Chile went up and wages sank lower. The wealthy, however, fared better than they had under Allende.

Toward the end of the 1970s, the economy rebounded. Foreign companies were welcomed, as well as foreign products. Chile had the lowest import tariffs in the world. Construction boomed, and wealthy Chileans enjoyed buying imported cars, clothing, and furniture. The poor were not entirely neglected. The government built low-income housing, improved sewers, and paved more streets. The end result, however, was a rapid concentration of wealth in the hands of a few individuals, among them—quite secretly—Augusto Pinochet himself.

"PROTECTED" DEMOCRACY

As the economy improved, Pinochet felt he had enough support to legitimize his dictatorship. For years he had been asked when democratic rule would return to Chile. In July 1977, he announced that he was ready to move Chile toward a "protected" democracy. He appointed his chief legal adviser, his cousin Mónica Madariaga, as his minister of justice, so that she could help him prove his regime was legitimate.

In March 1978, Pinochet declared an end to the "state of siege." It was replaced by a "state of emergency," which meant that cases to do with national security would be transferred from military to civilian courts. The curfew was finally lifted in April 1978. That year

STATES OF EXCEPTION

The constitution of 1980 gave Pinochet the right to suspend various civil rights under certain conditions determined by him. A "state of emergency" allowed him to impose a curfew and martial law (law administered by military forces instead of civilian law-enforcement agencies). A more drastic measure was a "state of siege," in which citizens could be imprisoned without a writ of habeas corpus (a document giving a lawful reason for arrest). Other rights, such as the right of assembly and the right to be free from unlawful searches, were suspended as well. Pinochet could also announce "a state of risk of disturbance of internal order" without giving a cause for doing so, or in the case of a severe natural disaster, such as the earthquake that struck Chile in March 1983, a "state of catastrophe." These provisions were designed to give legitimacy to Pinochet's dictatorial powers. During most of the seventeen years of Pinochet's rule, states of siege or emergency were in effect.

Pinochet also reorganized his cabinet to include more civilians. He began working out a plan for Chile's return to an elected government and assigning right-wing jurists to draft a constitution.

To "leave hatreds behind" and bring the nation together in a spirit of "peace and order," Pinochet issued an amnesty on all politically connected crimes committed between the coup and the end of the state of siege. The decree pardoned many leftist prisoners, most of whom were nevertheless sent into exile. It also freed

Pinochet, the military, and the police from being held responsible for the human rights abuses they had committed.

In 1980 Pinochet presented Chile with the new constitution. It stipulated that Pinochet would become the first president for one eight-year term. In 1988 the military government would choose a candidate to be president for the next eight years. Although later presidents would not be allowed to run for reelection, Pinochet had the right to be the candidate for the second term. The people would vote yes or no for this candidate chosen by the military in 1988. If the "no" vote won, then new presidential elections would be held. Either way, the first congressional elections would take place at that time.

Under the proposed constitution, when the new Congress convened, it would have limited powers. Nine out of the thirty-five senators would be appointed by the regime, not elected by the people. At least 80 percent of the senators had to approve any reform, which then had to pass the Chamber of Deputies with a vote of at least 65 percent.

Another feature of the constitution was that it gave the military a permanent role in the government. Officers representing the army, navy, air force, and national police were to serve on a National Security Council. The council could veto any legislation proposed by Congress. Since it had a total of seven voting members, the four military members held a majority. They could block any laws that might adversely affect the armed forces.

Pinochet was not planning to retire. Whatever the outcome of the "yes" or "no" vote in 1988, Pinochet would still be commander in chief of the army for ten more years. Then, according to the constitution, he would serve in Congress as a senator for the rest of his life.

Pinochet ordered a referendum of the new constitution to

establish its legitimacy. Chileans had a month to read and think about the document, but any opposition to it was given little chance to be heard. Former president Eduardo Frei spoke out against it, but since he had no access to television and the press, his appeal for a more democratic constitution reached few people.

Meanwhile, the government filled the airwaves and government newspapers with favorable propaganda. Pinochet pictured a rosy future in speeches he gave in support of the constitution. He promised to create one million new jobs and build nine thousand new homes. Every family in Chile would have a car, a color television, and a telephone.

On September 11, 1980, six million Chileans went to the polls. No registration of voters had taken place. People simply cast their votes at any polling site. To prevent double voting, each voter's right thumb was marked on an ink pad. The ink, however, was not indelible. Employees of the government or people who approved of it supervised the polls. These same people counted the votes. According to their count, 67 percent of the ballots were marked "yes." When the president of the Christian Democratic Party, Andrés Zaldívar, questioned the legitimacy of the plebiscite in the international press, Pinochet ordered him into exile for three years. "We have shown the world how democratic this nation is!" Pinochet boasted.

THE BUBBLE BURSTS

The year Chileans voted on the new constitution, the economic miracle began to waver. Economic growth was lower than that of the previous three years, and unemployment began to rise. By the next year, the economy was spiraling downward. Banks and other financial service companies were failing, and the government had to step in and take over. Many industries went bankrupt. By 1983 unemployment had soared to one-third of the workforce.

The poor were hit worst. Unemployment among young men in poor neighborhoods ran about 60 percent. Prices of bread, sugar, flour, and oil shot up. Many workers turned to selling chewing gum in the streets or cleaning the houses of the rich. A high-level banker told an interviewer: "The Central Bank took a hard line with us; we passed along the effects to our debtors; . . . our debtors . . . dismissed some of their workers and lowered the wages of others. . . . By means of this 'conveyor belt,' the pressure accumulated mainly in poor neighborhoods, where you find the overwhelming concentration of suffering created by this social volcano on which we now live."

The "social volcano" erupted on May 11, 1983. In response to a labor leader's call for a national day of

DESTITUTE CHILEANS STAND IN line at a soup kitchen. By 1983 thousands of homeless lived in squatter camps outside Santiago.

STUDENTS IN SANTIAGO FLEE A 1983 PROTEST AGAINST PINOCHET'S
regime as police officers spray them with a water cannon.

protest, Chileans surged into the streets, banging pots and pans and honking on car horns in a deafening demonstration against a government that had steadily reduced social services for the poor while rescuing wealthy businesses such as banks. Traffic and businesses in Santiago were paralyzed. It was a nonviolent demonstration, joined by many middle-class and upper-middle-class residents, but the government sent police and army units to disperse the crowds with clubs, water cannons, tear gas, and machine guns. Two demonstrators were killed, fifty were injured, and three hundred were arrested.

The people, however, did not give up. Four more mass protests took place over the next four months and more than twenty over the next three years.

Made bold by the mass demonstrations, political parties began to speak out against the military regime. Although political parties had been banned and many of their leaders executed or exiled, the major parties had never completely disappeared.

In July 1983, the Christian Democrats, the Socialists, and even the right-wing Republican Party, which had applauded the coup ten years earlier, joined forces to put pressure on the government for less censorship, less repression, and more democracy. Their founding document proclaimed: "As individuals with differing political, philosophical, and religious positions, we unite in agreeing to respect and promote certain ethical principles and values that democracy upholds, without which a free, prosperous, just, and fraternal society is not possible."

The Communist Party also made a strong return. Its leaders did not believe, however, that peaceful demonstrations would bring change to Chile. Instead, it formed a separate coalition with MIR and a faction of the Socialist Party that also advocated combating violence with violence. The Communists established a military arm known as the Manuel Rodríguez Patriotic Front (FPMR)—named for a hero in Chile's struggle for independence—and recruited frustrated and impoverished angry young men to fight in it and in paramilitary (auxiliary) forces.

Over the next three years, as the demonstrations and protests disrupted life in Santiago, Pinochet ordered more and more troops against the demonstrators. The confrontations became increasingly bloody. Casualties ran into the hundreds even by the official count. Once again, sports stadiums became holding pens for the large numbers of people arrested, most of them poor and unemployed. After the first few demonstrations in 1983, the middle and upper middle classes stayed away.

Through all the protests, Pinochet remained firm. "This is not

> *"I don't have confidence in orthodox democracy. It is too easy to infiltrate and destroy."*
>
> —Augusto Pinochet, 1984

a fascist government," he told television viewers in 1983. "It is a government that tries to protect the country from totalitarianism!" Nevertheless, he granted a few concessions to the democratic opposition. Book censorship was stopped, and civilian organizations were finally allowed to choose their own leaders. News and opinion magazines were occasionally permitted to publish opposition views. He even granted amnesty to some exiled Chileans, among them writers, artists, and non-Communist politicians. However small, these tokens of freedom were an improvement over what Chileans had faced since the coup.

A CLOSE CALL

The support Pinochet enjoyed during the economic boom was fast vanishing. The destructive skirmishes between the protesters and army troops horrified Chileans. Bands of Communist guerrillas blew up electric power lines, causing widespread outages. They stalled transportation by sabotaging railways and buses. In retaliation, army troops surrounded entire slum neighborhoods in the middle of the night, ordered residents out of their homes, and arrested all males over the age of fifteen.

On March 30, 1985, the bodies of three Communist leaders were found dumped on a roadside with their throats slashed. More than twenty thousand citizens defied "state of siege" orders to attend the funerals of the murdered men. A group of carabinero intelligence agents were later implicated in the killings. Because General Mendoza was in charge of the carabineros, the scandal prompted him to resign from the junta.

The increased violence and repression focused international attention on human rights abuses in Chile. U.S. policy toward Chile shifted. The U.S. Department of State replaced two officials who had been friendly to Pinochet, the ambassador to Chile and the assistant secretary of state responsible for U.S. relations with North and South American countries. Within Chile itself, eleven political groups presented Pinochet with new requests for an end to states of emergency, for presidential elections, and for a means of amending the constitution of 1980. Even the other junta members wished to discuss constitutional reforms. Pinochet refused to consider any changes.

As Pinochet approached his seventieth birthday in November 1985, people wondered how much longer he would be able to control the country. But he had no intention of stepping down. To assure the country of his vigor and health, he had television cameras record him doing his morning exercises on his birthday and had the tape broadcast for all Chileans to see.

The following September, as sporadic assaults by Communist commandos continued, Pinochet was returning to Santiago from his country home when armed guerrillas attacked his motorcade. Five of Pinochet's bodyguards were killed. Pinochet, however, escaped unharmed, saved by his armor-plated Mercedes and the failure of several of the attackers' missiles.

Pinochet declared yet another state of siege, and searches uncovered hidden arms caches. Within days the bodies of four known opponents of the dictatorship were found riddled with bullets. "Divine justice was on hand," Pinochet wrote in his memoirs.

The armed forces rallied behind their leader. For some Chileans, the situation reawakened old fears of a Communist takeover. Which was the worse evil, they wondered—Pinochet's dictatorship or Soviet-style Communism? Meanwhile, Chile's economy was beginning to improve, bringing more jobs. Pinochet's star seemed to be rising again.

PRO-PINOCHET DEMONSTRATORS PRESS AGAINST A POLICE LINE AT A rally in Santiago in 1986.

THE PLEBISCITE

After Pinochet's narrow escape and the renewed state of siege, leaders of the democratic opposition decided that their best hope was to work within Pinochet's 1980 plan for a transition to a "protected" democracy. As the time for the proposed 1988 plebiscite—to decide whether or not to accept the candidate chosen by the military—approached, they began to focus on defeating it.

In February 1987, the government began the process of registering voters. A month later, non-Marxist political parties were allowed to form by collecting thirty-five thousand signatures of registered voters. Several new parties emerged alongside the older ones. A year later, the opposition parties joined together in a *concertación* (agreement) to support a vote of "no" in the plebiscite.

Leaders of the opposition faced much harassment. Their campaign offices were firebombed and their rallies broken up by police. About two thousand political arrests occurred during the first six months of 1988. But members of the opposition still dared to speak out. The boldest was the Socialist leader Ricardo Lagos, who amazed the nation during a live television interview when he pointed his finger and looked directly into the camera to accuse Pinochet: "You promise the country eight more years of torture, assassination and human rights violations."

To no one's surprise, on August 30, the junta named Pinochet as the candidate who would become the transitional president if the "yes" vote won. The dictator felt fully confident that the majority of Chileans preferred the security and order of his regime to what his television campaign ads pictured as mob rule.

In September, opposition leaders persuaded the government

NO, NO, NO, NO, NO!
NO-NO! NO-NO!

In 1988 Florcita Motuda, a popular Chilean singer, recorded a version of Johann Strauss's "Blue Danube" waltz, singing only the word *no*. In addition to providing some comic relief in a difficult time, the song became one of the theme songs of the campaign. When the "no" vote won, crowds poured into the streets singing and dancing the "Imperial Waltz of No."

to allow them brief slots of television time, which they used well. Beginning September 5, "yes" and "no" political ads appeared for fifteen minutes between 10:45 P.M. and 11:15 P.M. on weeknights and between noon and 12:30 P.M. on weekends. Patricio Aylwin, the president of the Christian Democratic Party, acted as the spokesperson for the "no" coalition.

Pressure from the democratic opposition and also international opinion helped ensure that the election, unlike the plebiscite in 1980, would be fair. Even Pinochet's advisors believed that transparency would work in Pinochet's favor. Proper voting lists were prepared, every voter had to present voter registration and identity cards, and observers from both the government and the opposition parties watched the polls and counted the votes.

The vote took place on October 5, a date Pinochet chose after consulting a fortune-teller. He spent the day in a bunker he had built under the plaza facing La Moneda. He had "twenty-five thousand men ready" to protect him, he told reporters. That night, as voting results were slowly tallied, the first official announcements declared the "yes" votes were ahead. But the Chilean Air Force and Navy and the carabineros kept their own tallies, as did the "no" campaign.

These independent tallies showed the "no" vote was winning. By midnight, the news was out: "no" appeared to be ahead.

Pinochet was furious when the junta officers brought him the news. He thundered about using his emergency powers, but the junta reminded him he had sworn to uphold the constitution. Angry at what he called betrayals, he called in all his cabinet ministers and fired them.

When the final results were tabulated, "no" won 54.7 percent of the vote. Not until the next evening did Pinochet appear on television in his military uniform to admit defeat. "I recognize and accept the verdict expressed by a majority of citizens," he told Chileans. Still, he asserted his commitment "to the principles that inspired the glorious effort of September 11, 1973."

The constitution of 1980 gave Pinochet a year and a half to wind down his regime. Presidential and congressional elections would take place in December 1989. The new president of Chile would take office in March 1990. The seventeen years of Pinochet's dictatorship were almost over. But Pinochet was still in charge of the army, and laws still protected his dictatorship from prosecution. It would take many more years before Chile would be entirely free from Pinochet's control.

LIFE IN

THE LIVES OF CHILEAN CITIZENS CHANGED DRAMATICALLY when the junta overthrew Allende. Although the coup was quickly accomplished, with very little armed resistance, a state of siege was declared. On September 12, a twenty-four-hour curfew went into effect throughout Chile. Anyone on the streets risked being shot. Army trucks and tanks rumbled through towns and cities, and helicopters throbbed overhead. People heard gunfire and saw smoke.

The next day, civilians were allowed three hours, from noon to 3 P.M., to buy food and other necessities. The shelves were amazingly well stocked with bread, sugar, coffee, rice, oil, detergent, toilet paper, toothpaste—all the things it had been hard to find during the long strikes that preceded the coup. Shopkeepers, who had created shortages to hurt Allende, were ready to sell

the goods they had warehoused. However, they raised prices so people could not afford to buy much.

Gradually, life resumed. A less stringent curfew was announced—6 P.M. at first, then 8 P.M., and eventually later. The curfew remained in effect for years, although the government changed the time as it saw more or less danger to itself. In periods of relative quiet, the curfew lasted only from 1 or 2 A.M. to 5 A.M. When demonstrations began in 1983, longer curfews resumed. On days protests were scheduled, the government countered by declaring forty-eight-hour curfews. People became used to planning their lives so they would be indoors by whatever time the curfew went into effect. When curfew arrived, gunfire followed. Civilians at home did not know whether soldiers were firing their weapons as a warning or actually using them against people in the streets. That uncertainty became part of life in Pinochet's Chile.

LAW AND ORDER

Citizens noticed many differences in their environment after the coup. Buildings and walls in cities and along highways were quickly whitewashed to cover the slogans and murals of the Popular Unity movement. Vendors were banished from the streets. Bookstalls that were once stocked with popular magazines, and books of literature, philosophy, and politics were closed. Few people went to cafés or restaurants, and those who did conversed quietly as though fearful of being overheard. No one chatted while riding the buses, which carried warnings against writing anti-Pinochet slogans on the seat backs.

Nightlife, once it resumed, was similarly subdued. Radio stations played foreign music, not the Chilean protest ballads that were popular during the Frei and Allende years. Movies were preceded by newsreels featuring the latest junta decrees and activities. When the U.S. film *Cabaret* (a story set in Berlin in the 1930s) was shown in Chilean theaters, scenes showing Nazi soldiers in a negative light had been removed.

SOLDIERS REMOVE GRAFFITI favoring the Popular Unity movement from a wall in Santiago.

The most obvious change was the constant military presence. In every neighborhood, armed, uniformed soldiers patrolled the streets in twos and threes. Small armored vehicles stood at every corner, with busloads of reinforcements parked nearby. Every day, military motorcades sped through Santiago and other cities, tying up civilian traffic at unpredictable times. Military men ran universities, prisons, factories, villages, and cities. They stood guard in libraries, schools, supermarkets, newspaper offices, publishing houses, and theaters. It was as though Chile was an occupied country, only the occupying force was Chilean.

Not every Chilean experienced this military occupation in the same way. How Chileans felt about Pinochet's regime depended a great deal on their social class, their political sympathies, and their employment—or lack of it.

"After [the curfew], leaving the house was impossible. You couldn't even peek out the door because police patrols started in my neighborhood, forcing everyone to remain inside. At nightfall there was surveillance by copters and land vehicles, and you heard shooting, ceaselessly, small caliber arms against big ones, especially machine guns."

—Eduardo Creus, Argentine journalist in Chile, 1973

DARK HUMOR

Chileans are known for making witty jokes even in the face of disasters. Living in Pinochet's Chile was no exception.

"Did you hear about the new bus line?" began one joke that circulated in late 1973.

"No, where does it go?"

"From the National Stadium to the cemetery."

Another goes: "General Pinochet went to the movies disguised as an old lady so that he could see how many people clapped when he appeared on the screen in the newsreel. He sat entranced as people applauded his image until his neighbor nudged him and said, 'Clap you silly old fool, or they'll shoot you.'"

A popular cartoon addressed the difficulties people faced proving their innocence. It showed a rabbit hopping away from elephant hunters, saying, "How can I convince them I am not an elephant?"

THE ENFORCERS OF ORDER

Members of the military and the police found themselves playing a much more important role in society under Pinochet. Their activities also embraced a much wider range than previously. Instead of being isolated in their barracks and bases training for war and engaging in war games when no war threatened Chile, soldiers had assignments that they were told were essential to Chile's national security. Earlier the military's only civilian task was overseeing polling sites during elections. But during the dictatorship, soldiers went on daily patrols throughout the country, enforcing curfews, searching areas suspected of harboring enemies or weapons, and guarding detainees. The carabineros' role changed less, but like the soldiers, their activities and powers increased.

Pinochet made certain of the soldiers' loyalty by rewarding them with benefits. They enjoyed stable employment, free housing, and education for their children. Their neighborhoods, set apart from civilian areas, had their own well-stocked and reasonably priced shopping centers. They were also well paid. Military officers earned three or four times the income of civilians. By 1989, for example, army colonels received 191,000 pesos a month and captains 146,000. A veteran teacher or civil engineer, on the other hand, earned only about 50,000 pesos a month. The military became a separate society, more privileged than average Chileans.

Not all the military and police favored the violent overthrow of the democratically elected government. They believed that their role was to help the government maintain order and to defend it, not to wage war against it. Military discipline, however, made it difficult for them to go against the orders of their superiors. Soldiers who dared to express their objections risked being executed for treason.

One young army corporal, horrified at being ordered to beat detainees, decided to escape from the army by being arrested. When he had a one-day pass, he joined a street fight and resisted the soldiers who came to break it up. He was arrested for disorderly conduct and illegal possession of a weapon—someone had placed a pistol in his pocket—and spent almost a year in jail before being released. But he felt the experience was worthwhile. His conviction freed him from having to serve in the army.

Officers who had opposed the coup or did not participate in it were arrested, beaten, and tortured. One victim was General

Alberto Bachelet, who died following a heart attack after repeated interrogations and torture. Another was the general who commanded the army's mountain training school. Pinochet had sent his wife and younger children there for safety on September 10 because he knew the general would remain loyal to the government. The general died mysteriously a few days after the coup.

Some officers who supported the coup and worked for the junta eventually became disillusioned by the continuous violence and repression. General Oscar Bonilla, Pinochet's defense minister, and General Augusto Lutz, secretary to the junta, appealed privately to

GENERAL OSCAR BONILLA, THE JUNTA'S MINISTER OF DEFENSE, TOURS a slum outside Santiago. His appeals for an end to kidnappings and torture put him out of favor with Pinochet.

Pinochet to stop DINA's vicious and unlawful torture and killings. Both later died in suspicious circumstances, Lutz apparently poisoned and Bonilla in an army helicopter crash.

CIVILIAN LIFE

The increased presence of the military and the police affected civilian life in several ways. Wealthy homeowners, who lived behind tall walls in the hilly neighborhoods overlooking city centers, felt fairly safe. Poor, unemployed workers in the shantytowns on city outskirts felt intimidated. Often the nighttime gunfire overheard in well-to-do areas was a raid on a poor neighborhood.

These raids were never reported in the press, so people living in other neighborhoods knew little about them. If they heard rumors, these often came from people they did not particularly trust. The gulf between rich and poor—and between liberal and conservative views—was possibly the deepest it had ever been in Chilean society.

Many people turned inward and kept to themselves, trusting only close family members or their oldest friends. They tried to live as though everything were normal, a strategy that came to be called "submarining." Fearful of saying the wrong thing, they learned to "sniff" their neighbors or people they met at parties, asking casual questions about their reading, where they lived, what they did for a living to determine indirectly whether they were for or against the regime.

One professor told a journalist in the mid-1980s, "We have lost the capacity to feel the suffering of our neighbor as if it were our own.

We are not moved by the suffering of another person. Perhaps not even moved by our own suffering. Chileans no longer feel anything."

ARREST, TORTURE, DEATH

Those who suffered most during Pinochet's dictatorship were the victims of human rights abuse and political violence, as well as the families and friends who mourned their loss. According to later tabulations, the number of deaths between 1973 and 1990 caused by the coup and the repression that followed was 3,197. Of these, only 173 deaths were of members of the armed forces, the carabineros, and the civil police. The rest were civilians, often killed after torture and beating, and with no legal charges against them.

"They had a barometer: it was that blood would burst from my nose and ears. I noticed that when I felt something hot drip from my nose and ears, they would calm down and lower me."

—actor Sergio Buschmann, explaining how he was blindfolded, hung, and beaten every day for sixteen days

About half of those victims lost their lives in the three and a half months following the coup in 1973. Many died during the next four years, when DINA was active. Most of the rest were killed during the economic crisis and protests of the mid-1980s.

Most of the victims were young men between the ages of sixteen and thirty. More than one third worked in factories or mines or labored on farms. Almost half belonged to one of the political parties that made up Allende's Popular Unity. For a large number of victims, the political affiliation is unknown. Almost four hundred were students, but others were shopkeepers, doctors, lawyers, teachers, public employees, farmers, and housewives. Eighty were children and young teens.

Countless thousands of relatives were effected, some searching desperately for years before learning the truth. Adding to their pain, many never knew why or how their loved ones died and never had the chance to bury and mourn them. They were further haunted by the knowledge that the victims were probably tortured.

Many victims of the government's repression survived, and their testimony has been collected and published. Large numbers of people were arrested and illegally detained. According to the 2004 report of an official commission investigating torture during the seventeen years of Pinochet's dictatorship, about twenty-eight thousand people were tortured. Most were men, but at least thirty-four hundred of them were women.

These facts came to light only after Pinochet's dictatorship ended. During his rule, the lack of accurate knowledge at times led to exaggerated estimates of what was going on. These rumors added to the fears of those who felt vulnerable. They also reassured Pinochet's supporters that such things could not really be happening.

LIVING IN EXILE

For an estimated 450,000 Chileans, life in Chile was no longer possible under the dictatorship. Some chose to leave their homes and their country. Fearing they would be arrested for their political sympathies, they fled, driving over the border into Argentina or begging for asylum at an embassy or consulate—a friendly one, as not all foreign diplomats were willing to help refugees.

Many, however, had no choice. They were ordered to leave. The lucky ones had a few hours to pack before they were picked up and taken to the airport. Some were arrested, driven to the border, and released without personal belongings or even documents. Others had their passports stamped with an *L* for *listado* (listed), which ensured that no border guard or immigration officer would permit them to reenter Chile legally.

In the first two years after the coup, about fourteen thousand Chileans were granted diplomatic asylum in many different countries around the world. By 1979 the figure had reached thirty thousand. Sweden accepted more than five thousand Chilean refugees, France more than three thousand. Italy, the Netherlands, Great Britain, and Canada also took in Chilean exiles. Some members of the Communist and Socialist parties went to Communist countries, such as Cuba, the Soviet Union, East Germany, or Romania. Large numbers found refuge in other Latin American countries—Mexico, Brazil, Venezuela, Argentina—or in Spain. The United States, in contrast, issued only twenty-five visas to Chilean exiles, although it received one hundred forty requests.

A few committed revolutionaries joined guerrilla forces in Argentina and Nicaragua or trained in guerrilla tactics in Cuba,

Eastern Europe, and northern Africa. They then slipped back into Chile to enlist in MIR or the FPMR. Most exiles, however, lived quiet lives of waiting. Feeling estranged, isolated, and homeless, many small communities of exiles hung closely together, living mainly in the past, as they worked at whatever jobs they could find and struggled to adjust to new customs and sometimes new languages. Some exiles campaigned in their new countries to awaken international opposition to Pinochet's regime. Some even testified before the United Nations (UN) about human rights abuses, risking harassment or worse from DINA agents.

For the majority, their exile lasted at least a decade. Only in 1982 did the government begin publishing lists, a hundred or so names at a time, of those allowed to return. Thinking it would help him win votes in the 1988 plebiscite, Pinochet declared that all Chileans still in exile were free to come home. Allende's widow, Hortensia Bussi, was among many who returned at that time and joined the campaign for "no."

HORTENSIA BUSSI (RIGHT), THE WIDOW OF SALVADOR ALLENDE, WAS ONE of the exiles allowed to return to Chile in the late 1980s.

For some exiles, returning was almost as hard as leaving. Chile had changed, and old ties had broken. Former exiles once again had to restart their lives, find work and housing, and adjust to a more modern country than the one they had left many years earlier. A number of former exiles helped lead the transition to democracy, among them the Socialist politician Ricardo Lagos.

RESISTING AND PROTESTING

In spite of the repression, many citizens who remained in Chile found ways to avoid being intimidated. They worked together to help those being persecuted by the military regime.

One institution that the military did not take over was the Catholic Church. Soon after the coup, Cardinal Raúl Silva, the archbishop of Santiago, together with Protestant and Jewish religious leaders, formed a Committee for Peace. The committee gave sanctuary, spiritual comfort, and legal aid to people whose lives were in danger. Many lay people—lawyers, professors, doctors, and psychologists—assisted the Peace Committee with their skills, even at the risk of being exiled or imprisoned (as several were). The committee helped more than five thousand refugees leave Chile safely before Pinochet ordered its dissolution in late 1975.

In January 1976, the archbishop formed a new organization within the Roman Catholic Church to replace the committee. Since it was part of the church, the government could not easily interfere with its activities. Known as the Vicariate of Solidarity, the new organization helped victims of torture and played a valuable role in keeping records of the crimes committed by Pinochet's dictatorship. As Chile's economy worsened and the junta cut back on social services, the vicariate also opened soup kitchens to feed the poor and unemployed.

After the universities were placed under military administration, dissident students and faculty members carried on with academic work by creating underground communities. Ousted professors taught expelled students in secret and raised funds for scholarships canceled by the dictatorship. Out-of-work scholars continued to do research and kept in touch with colleagues outside the country. These communications were an important source of uncensored information for the world outside Chile.

More active protests against Pinochet's dictatorship began during the 1980s. By 1981 groups of women—mothers and wives of the "disappeared"—were staging sit-ins in front of La Moneda. Each woman carried at least one photograph of a disappeared relative or pinned a picture to her blouse. Some had as many as four or five. "Where are they?" posters asked. Unfazed by arrests and time in prison, they returned again and again to publicize their losses.

WOMEN RAISE PICTURES OF MISSING LOVED ONES AT A 1983 PROTEST IN
Santiago. Each picture is labeled *"¿Dónde están?"* or "Where are they?"

In the mid-1980s, when the economic downturn brought wider dissatisfaction with the dictatorship, Chileans took to the streets. The first mass demonstration in 1983 was joined by many middle- and upper-class people who had earlier supported the coup. When the government tried to prevent these expressions of discontent by declaring forty-eight-hour curfews, protesters stayed home but leaned out their windows to wave banners and bang pots and pans.

A more ominous and destructive resistance by militant Communists later undermined the peaceful, nonviolent mass demonstrations. Their attempt to assassinate Pinochet in 1986 effectively put an end to large protests and marches. Smaller groups, however, continued to stage brief demonstrations. Choosing a busy street with many passersby, they would quickly unfurl banners printed with information about human rights abuses and stand silently pointing at government buildings.

THOUGHT CONTROL

From the beginning, the members of the military junta pictured their role as liberators who were freeing Chile from a dangerous enemy. Cuba and the Soviet Union, they claimed, were intent on overthrowing democracy and establishing a totalitarian Communist government in Chile. Allende's stated goal of achieving a more egalitarian and more democratic society through a peaceful, constitutional process, they argued, was a lie he was using to gain support and to cover up his real goal.

As proof that Communists were threatening to take over Chile, in October 1973, the military regime published a justification of the coup called the *Libro Blanco* (White Book). It gave details of an alleged Socialist plot, code-named Plan Z, to assassinate senior military officials and civilian leaders who opposed Popular Unity. The plan, it asserted, had been scheduled for the patriotic holidays of September 18 (Chile's Independence Day) and September 19 (Armed Forces Day), when all the military leaders would be in Santiago for the celebrations. The White Book also stated that between ten and fifteen thousand foreigners, trained in guerrilla fighting and well supplied with weapons, were already in Chile. Many Chileans, especially those in the military, believed these frightening fabrications were true.

To prevent the publication or broadcast of information that contradicted the dictatorship, the regime appointed a censor to every Chilean newspaper, magazine, television station, and radio station. Books that the junta considered subversive were destroyed in public bonfires. When the Nobel Prize-winning Chilean poet and Communist Party activist Pablo Neruda died of cancer shortly after the coup, his vast book collection was vandalized. Even novels by Latin American authors Gabriel García Márquez and Mario Vargas Llosa were banned, not because the books were considered dangerous but because the authors had spoken out against the military regime.

Conservative newspapers helped the dictatorship. "Our idea was to be critical collaborators," an editor of *El Mercurio* said, "to be loyal to the government but to warn them about especially bad things." Pinochet, however, disliked even mild criticism. When *El Mercurio* criticized the murder of a union leader in 1982, the editor was fired and replaced by a *pinochetista* (Pinochet supporter).

The most effective propaganda weapon for the dictatorship was television, which reached far more people than newspapers and books. Taking over state-owned Channel 7, the only channel that had a nationwide network, the regime broadcast soap operas, military parades, soccer games, and variety shows. News programs consisted of official announcements, ministers cutting ribbons at new housing projects, stories of leftist violence, and Pinochet making speeches. The dictator was not a polished speaker, so he was usually shown without sound, while a voice-over paraphrased what he said.

WINNING LOYALTY

To carry out Pinochet's desire for a "moral cleansing" and a "change in mentality," organizations for women and youth were formed. Pinochet's wife Lucía Hiriart led an army of twenty thousand volunteer middle-class housewives. They dressed alike in pink or lilac smocks. As one of the women explained, "a uniform lessens the distance" between their own privileged lives and those of the poor that they set out to help. By aiding the elderly and teaching poor women crafts, these women hoped to gain supporters for the dictatorship as well as promote family values and respect for authority.

Pinochet took a personal interest in winning the loyalty of young people. Summer camps and neighborhood clubs provided sports and recreation as well as political indoctrination and vocational training. Military-style awards and medals encouraged civilian-military ties. In 1975 a Youth Day was established. It was set for July 9, a day already celebrated by the military to commemorate the Battle of La Concepción, fought in Peru during the War of the Pacific in 1881. Every year large rallies in several cities brought thousands of civilian youths, cadets, and military officers together for torchlit parades and pro-regime speeches.

A new school curriculum that focused on "the concepts of love of God, the Fatherland and the family" was announced in the *National Objectives of the Chilean Government* issued in 1975. Five years later, the universities were being overhauled. Departments of philosophy, social and political science, humanities, and arts were abolished. Universities were prohibited to "foment actions or conduct" that disrupted public order or to "propagate directly or indirectly" partisan politics. Universities were ordered to become financially self-supporting. Formerly free, higher education became an expensive investment that only the wealthy could afford. Courses of study were limited to such fields as business management, computer programming, engineering, medicine, and dentistry.

The protests of the mid-1980s brought some relaxation of the censorship rules. Publishers no longer needed to have manuscripts approved by the ministry of the interior. Books by former political prisoners began to reveal grim details of torture and murder perpetrated by the military regime. New magazines appeared on newsstands, but their publishers often faced harassment for what they printed. Deciding what was allowed was "a constant, dangerous ballet," one editor commented. When one magazine printed a cartoon of Pinochet as totalitarian King Louis XIV of France on its cover, its two editors spent two months in jail.

But the dictatorship's battle for Chilean hearts and minds was losing ground. In 1986 the first opposition newspaper appeared. In 1988 the democratic opposition at last won the right to express their views on national television. Even though it was only fifteen minutes a day—and on weekdays scheduled at 11 P.M.—large numbers of Chileans stayed up and tuned in. The results of the plebiscite on October 5 proved Pinochet's failure to convince the majority of Chileans that he was the liberating hero of their country.

CHAPTER 5

CHILE AND THE

THE MILITARY COUP THAT BEGAN PINOCHET'S RISE TO POWER was
noted around the world. Enough information had spread about the
paralyzing strikes and growing political unrest in Chile that news
watchers were not entirely surprised. Reactions to the coup generally reflected the political divisions that brought it about.

Most Communist countries—the USSR, Cuba, Yugoslavia, and
countries in Eastern Europe—condemned the coup at once. The
People's Republic of China was the only exception. It was the
first foreign government to establish diplomatic relations with
the new regime.

Countries with Socialist governments or strong leftist parties
expressed disapproval, but most stopped short of breaking off
diplomatic relations. Sweden, Italy, and the Netherlands recalled
their ambassadors. Thousands of Europeans protested the coup,

OUTSIDE WORLD

THOUSANDS OF ITALIANS MARCHED THROUGH THE STREETS OF ROME ON
September 12, 1973, protesting against the coup in Chile. The poster shows Allende.

marching in parades or holding rallies in Paris, France; Rome, Italy; Hamburg, Munich, and Frankfurt, Germany; and Brussels, Belgium.

Within Latin America, other countries with military dictatorships—Brazil, Uruguay, Paraguay, and Peru—welcomed Chile's new regime. Democracies such as Mexico, Venezuela, and Colombia held back.

The United States also held back at first. President Nixon's administration generally preferred military governments in Latin America because they were anti-Communist. Democratically elected governments too often threatened to seize the investments of U.S. citizens and corporations.

"The United States Government is so big and so powerful that our actions become that much more significant," a State Department official explained to a *New York Times* reporter. "Therefore we will try to make taking up relations not significant in the timing, to glide in, so to speak—not the first and not the last—so that no one can infer a special meaning."

The "special meaning" the Nixon administration did not want people to "infer" was that the United States had played an active role in the coup. The United States delayed in recognizing the junta for two weeks (by then, twenty-two other countries had done so), but what the State Department called their "hands-off" policy did not convince anyone. Around the world and even in the United States, large numbers of people were blaming the United States or its CIA for aiding the coup.

HELPING REFUGEES

Even before the governments of other nations had a chance to decide on what position to take concerning the military junta, their ambassadors and consuls in Chile had to take action right away. Most of the military activity on September 11 centered on La Moneda, but other units were sent out to attack and bomb Allende's residence, Socialist and Communist Party headquarters, and the Cuban Embassy.

When the Swedish ambassador, Harald Edelstam, who lived near the Cuban Embassy, saw what was happening there, he marched over and challenged the army troops. The grounds of a foreign embassy belong to the country that sends its representatives there. The host country has no right to attack or seize an embassy. To do so is an act of war against that country. Reminded of this by the Swedish envoy, the troops withheld their fire. The army captain leading the assault sent for advice. A message came from the junta stating that all Cuban personnel were to be expelled from Chile and would be taken to Santiago's Pudahuel Airport that night. A Soviet airliner rescued the Cubans and flew them to Havana, Cuba. Allende's daughter, Beatriz, who was married to the Cuban diplomat Luís Fernández de Oña, left with them.

The Swedish ambassador hung a Swedish flag on the Cuban Embassy to prevent troops from seizing the building. It was now Swedish territory, he declared. The embassy then became another haven for many political activists and their families. Until Sweden broke off diplomatic relations with Chile, Edelstam helped more than a thousand refugees get safely out of Chile.

Several other embassies also gave asylum to the refugees, their gardens soon crammed with tents full of frightened people. Allende's widow, Hortensia Bussi, took shelter in the Mexican Embassy after the Allende home was bombed. Various disguises and tricks were used to spirit people to safety. These included false names, false beards, cross-dressing—whatever it took to sneak people into the international territory of a sympathetic embassy and from there to an airport. The embassies of France, the Netherlands, Belgium, and Venezuela were among those that responded to the need. The embassy of the United States was not. Not only were no Chileans sheltered from the violence, the embassy even turned away some U.S. citizens who came for help.

NIXON, KISSINGER, AND FORD

The question of U.S. involvement in the coup was debated for decades. The Chile Declassification Project, which assembled about twenty-four thousand never-before-published U.S. documents in 1999–2000, pinned down some answers. The documents indicate that the CIA was not directly involved. It did not provide plans, equipment, personnel, or guarantees of U.S. help for a coup. But it does show that the CIA and other U.S. government groups were very active in operations intended to create a "coup climate"—a chaotic situation designed to encourage the overthrow of Chilean democracy. The Nixon administration also made certain that the armed forces of Chile were aware of U.S. anti-Allende views.

U.S. policy toward Chile made a U-turn once Allende was overthrown. When after months of rumors, the coup finally occurred, the Nixon administration was clearly pleased. "Our policy on Allende worked very well," Jack Kubisch, the assistant secretary of state for inter-American affairs, commented to Kissinger on September 12. While openly withholding recognition of the new regime, the State Department secretly notified the junta on September 13: "The USG [U.S. government] wishes to make clear its desire to cooperate with the military junta and to assist in any appropriate way."

The Nixon administration saw to it that economic aid to Chile, blocked during the Allende government, was quickly restored. For the next three years, generous multimillion dollar credits to relieve food shortages, housing grants, and loans from the World Bank and the Inter-American Development Bank flowed to Chile. According to declassified State Department records, these were all intended to "maintain and strengthen" Pinochet's dictatorship. Much of the money went to buy weapons and other military equipment—tanks, supersonic fighter aircraft, missiles, jeeps, submachine guns, rifles, ammunition, antiriot gear, and communications and air defense systems.

News of Pinochet's brutal repression, however, made it difficult for the Nixon administration to support the coup openly. Secretly, the United States provided flares and steel helmets for military operations as well as tents and blankets for detention camps. "However unpleasant they act," Secretary of State Kissinger reminded Kubisch, "this government is better for us than Allende was."

Also covertly, the CIA worked to secure support for Pinochet's dictatorship both inside Chile and abroad. CIA collaborators helped the junta draft the White Book with its allegations of Communist subversion in Chile. Secret CIA funds paid for a group of prominent Christian Democratic politicians to make a tour of Latin America and Europe explaining the reasons for the coup. At the time, these Chilean political leaders still believed the military regime was only a temporary measure to restore order in Chile.

The role the CIA played in planning and organizing the DINA and training DINA agents is still almost entirely top secret. By reading between the blacked-out lines and paragraphs, however, one can see that the CIA was closely involved with the DINA chief, Colonel (later General) Manuel Contreras, and was fully aware of the human rights abuses in Chile. Contreras was even paid as a CIA asset (spy or paid informer).

The CIA was also aware of the arrangements the regime was making to share information with the intelligence agencies of neighboring military dictatorships in South America. Proposed by Pinochet in 1975, Operation Condor was a secret alliance among the security services of Chile, Bolivia, Brazil, Paraguay, Uruguay, and Argentina. The stated goal of the operation was "to eliminate

Marxist terrorist activities" with "special teams which travel any-where in the world with sanctions up to assassination against terrorists or supporters of terrorist organizations." The wording suggests Condor was being organized to defeat the bands of left-ist guerrillas—inspired by Marx and the Argentine-born revolu-tionary Ernesto "Che" Guevara—who were trying to undermine several military regimes in Latin America.

But Pinochet's aim was to use Operation Condor against all his opponents, including nonviolent individuals and groups who were protesting human rights abuses in Chile. Operation Condor would extend the reach of the DINA by means of an international network of spies and assassins. In effect, Operation Condor was itself a ter-rorist organization.

Unlike the Republican-led White House and State Department, Democrats in Congress were not as welcoming of the military regime. On September 12, 1973, reports from Santiago of the arrests of thousands of political refugees from Brazil, Argentina, and other Latin American countries reached the United States. These people had been granted asylum by Allende's government. To ensure their safety, Democratic senator Edward Kennedy of Massachusetts immediately appealed to the UN High Commissioner for Refugees on their behalf. It was the first of many efforts by Democrats to com-bat the military repression in Chile.

By December 1973, the U.S. Congress was holding hearings on human rights abuses in Chile. An observer sent to Chile by the human rights organization Amnesty International reported wide-spread evidence of detentions without charges, torture, and arbi-trary killings. Persistent questions about the role of the CIA in Chile later led to Senate hearings chaired by Senator Frank Church of Idaho. The publication of the committee's findings about secret CIA

PINOCHET *(LEFT)* **AND ARGENTINE DICTATOR GENERAL JORGE VIDELA** *(RIGHT)* agreed to share intelligence as part of Operation Condor.

attempts to control Chilean politics between 1963 and 1973 created a public debate about the ethics of such actions.

A turning point in U.S. relations with Chile came in 1976. Early that year, Kennedy introduced legislation that finally ended U.S. arms sales and military assistance to Pinochet's dictatorship and set a limit on economic aid as well. In September the murder of former Chilean ambassador, Orlando Letelier, and his assistant Ronni Moffitt, in Washington, D.C., further aroused anti-Pinochet sentiment. In November, Democratic candidate Jimmy Carter defeated Republican incumbent Gerald Ford in the presidential elections. During the campaign, Carter had described the Republican White House under Nixon and Ford as an administration that "overthrew an elected government and helped establish a military dictatorship [in Chile]."

For the next four years, the White House and the State Department turned a cold shoulder to the Pinochet regime. After years of abstaining from the vote, the United States finally joined the majority when the UN voted to condemn Chile for human rights abuses. The Carter administration established a bureau of human rights within the State Department to report annually on the human rights record of each country being given aid by the United States. Later, the report was expanded to include every country in the world. The U.S. government began inviting Chilean politicians who opposed the Pinochet dictatorship to Washington.

The aid cutbacks by the U.S. Congress were not especially hurtful to the Chilean economy. Chile continued to get loans from private banks, as well as from the World Bank and the Inter-American Development Bank. As Pinochet commented to his inner circle, "The rejection of the White House and Capitol Hill does not matter as long as my government gets along well with Wall Street." Nor

FLIP-FLOPPING ON PINOCHET

The United States was not the only country to change its view of Pinochet's dictatorship. Great Britain recalled its ambassador in 1975 after Sheila Cassidy, a British doctor working in Chile, was arrested and tortured for giving medical aid to a wounded Communist guerrilla. When Margaret Thatcher became the British prime minister in 1979, was the U.S. arms embargo a problem for Pinochet. Chile began purchasing weapons from Israel, France, and South Africa. It also began manufacturing its own.

But the pressure from the United States and the international community on human rights abuses probably did contribute to changes in Pinochet's dictatorship. In late 1976, the military regime announced the release of 304 political prisoners. They were immediately expelled from the country, but at least they were free from imprisonment. In 1977 two notorious detention centers were closed. The DINA was replaced by the CNI. Although torture and mass detentions continued, incidents of "disappearances" and assassinations outside Chile dropped off sharply. In 1978 the state of siege ended, the curfew was lifted, amnesty declared (although this measure helped Pinochet more than it did his political opposition), and work began on a new constitution, even though it was a very conservative one.

DISPUTES WITH NEIGHBORS

Chile's relationships with neighboring countries also deteriorated in the late 1970s. In March 1978, Bolivia broke off relations with Chile as part of an ongoing effort to regain access to the Pacific Ocean. Bolivia had lost its coastline in the War of the Pacific a century earlier. In 1979 Bolivia secured the support of the Organization of American States, an international organization that promotes social and economic development in the Western hemisphere through cooperation. The dispute, however, remained unsettled.

Relations with Argentina were strained as well, and it is possible that Bolivia and Peru were secretly ready to back Argentina in any conflict it had with Chile. An old dispute between Chile and Argentina surfaced in 1978. It concerned three small, uninhabited islands in the Beagle Channel, which connects the Atlantic and Pacific oceans south of the island of Tierra del Fuego. Several years earlier, the two countries had agreed to British arbitration. When Queen Elizabeth II awarded the islands to Chile, however, the military junta in Argentina refused to accept the decision. The two countries were about to go to war over the issue when the newly elected pope John Paul II offered to mediate the conflict. The two nations agreed to maintain peace during the negotiations.

Intent on consolidating his power at home, Pinochet made few trips outside Chile after the coup, although in the 1970s, he did attend the inauguration of the president of Brazil and the funeral of the Spanish dictator Francisco Franco. He was the only head of state to attend the funeral. He joined other heads of North and South American states in Washington, D.C., for the signing of the Panama Canal Treaty in 1977.

PINOCHET *(LEFT)* AND LUCÍA HIRIART SPEAK WITH SPANISH KING JUAN CARLOS *(right)* during a visit to Madrid, Spain, for the funeral of Francisco Franco in 1975.

Pinochet longed to gain international recognition as the legitimate ruler of Chile. Leaving the country on a state visit would prove that his regime was not totally isolated from the rest of the world. In March 1980, he set out on his first major state visit abroad. President Ferdinand Marcos of the Philippines and his wife Imelda had invited the Pinochets to Manila. The two heads of state would discuss trade, Pinochet would be awarded an honorary degree, and the visit would end with a state banquet with the French, West German, and U.S. ambassadors among the guests.

The journey included a stopover in Fiji, where Pinochet planned to meet with the prime minister of that island republic. Just before they landed in Suva, Fiji, however, a message reached the aircraft that the Manila visit was canceled. International pressure, especially from Sweden, as well as the threat of demonstrations by Philippine church groups and unions, had persuaded the Philippine government to call off the meeting.

Adding to Pinochet's embarrassment and humiliation, demonstrators pelted the Pinochets' car with tomatoes and eggs as they went to spend the night at a hotel in Suva. The prime minister of Fiji also canceled his meeting with Pinochet, and the next day, the Pinochets flew back to Chile.

REAGAN AND PINOCHET

When Ronald Reagan became president in 1981, the United States renewed its support of Pinochet's dictatorship. Reagan backed Pinochet for much the same reasons Nixon had.

The Cold War was not over. Communist aggression was an

> *"Many of the workers and the unemployed rightly felt that Reagan's victory would strengthen Pinochet's hold on their country. I saw people with anguished faces burst into tears. Reagan's election was a hard blow to all of us. Chileans feel that Pinochet, at a minimum, has won a possible four-year reprieve."*
>
> —Maria B., in Valparaíso, Chile, 1980

ongoing threat, as the Soviet Union had proved with its invasion of Afghanistan two years earlier.

Reagan believed "friendly dictatorships" were a useful barrier to the spread of Soviet-style Communism. Economic and military aid once again began to flow from the United States to Chile. Shared naval maneuvers resumed between the United States and Chilean navies. Although the UN Human Rights Commission reported an increase in arbitrary arrests and detentions in 1981, the United States, along with the military governments of Argentina, Brazil, and Uruguay, went back to voting against UN resolutions that punished Chile.

For a time, the Pinochet dictatorship seemed on its way to gaining wider acceptance and recognition. General Fernando Matthei, the air force officer who had replaced General Leigh on the junta, was invited to Washington, D.C., and high-ranking U.S. diplomats visited Chile. These included Jeane Kirkpatrick, Reagan's ambassador to the UN, and General Vernon Walters, Reagan's ambassador-at-large (an ambassador who is not assigned to a specific country).

THE FALKLANDS WAR

Negotiations concerning the Beagle Channel islands were still going on when the Argentine junta, intent on gaining control of the South Atlantic, came up with a new plan. In April 1982, to everyone's surprise, Argentina invaded the Falkland Islands (known in Spanish as Islas Malvinas), a British colony in the South Atlantic Ocean, 300 miles (480 km) east of mainland Argentina.

The British, 8,000 miles (12,875 km) away, were hard pressed to organize a rescue for their colony. However, the Conservative Party-led government of Margaret Thatcher had reestablished relations with Chile when it came to power in 1979. The British turned to Chile for logistical help in the war. In exchange for sophisticated airplanes, missiles, and radar, the Chilean Air Force

ARGENTINE TROOPS STAND READY WITH AN ANTI-AIRCRAFT GUN ON THE coast of one of the Falkland Islands.

provided landing sites for British reconnaissance flights. It also supplied communications facilities that enabled the British to evade Argentine air defense as they sailed toward the islands. The Chilean Navy may also have informed the British about the locations of Argentine ships.

The British victory in the Falklands War helped Chile considerably. Argentina's military junta was brought down by the defeat, and for a while, hostilities between the two neighboring countries cooled off. Chile's aid to Great Britain, meanwhile, was kept secret until the end of the century. Although no formal treaty was signed between their two nations, Thatcher became a staunch ally of Pinochet.

During the 1980s, as Chileans protested Pinochet's dictatorship and harsh repression increased in Chile, Reagan began to speak out for a return to democracy there. On Human Rights Day, December 10, 1984, Reagan said that the lack of progress toward democracy in Chile was "an affront to human consciences." In response, Pinochet angrily told three members of the U.S. Congress visiting Santiago, "Don't stick your nose in affairs that don't concern you."

The following year, Reagan appointed a new ambassador to Chile, as well as a new assistant secretary of state for inter-American affairs in the State Department. Both replaced officials who had sympathized with Pinochet. The new ambassador opened dialogues with opposition politicians in Chile and with the Vicariate of Solidarity, the Catholic organization that helped victims and reported on cases of human rights abuse.

As Chilean political parties joined forces to win the 1988 plebiscite, the U.S. government and private citizens helped the opposition with organizing voter registration and training Chilean leaders in election monitoring. Political consultants from the

HOLLYWOOD ACTOR CHRISTOPHER

Reeve visited Chile to encourage participation in the "no" campaign.

United States volunteered their expertise. Hollywood stars Jane Fonda and Christopher Reeve joined leading Chilean actors and public figures to make ads for the "no" campaign.

Other countries also joined the effort to oust Pinochet peacefully with a show of democratic, not military, power. On the day of the vote, October 5, 1988, fifteen hundred foreign observers and reporters were on hand to help ensure that Chileans had the chance to vote freely and fairly. After fifteen years of living in a dictatorship, Chileans were beginning to see a light at the end of a very long tunnel.

CHAPTER 6

DISMANTLING

AFTER THE "NO" VICTORY, CHILEANS POURED OUT into the streets to express their jubilation. It was spring, a time of hope. In Santiago thousands of Chileans wanted the change to be immediate. Shaking their fists and shouting, "Pinochet, Out!" they surged toward La Moneda. Political leaders urged citizens to celebrate at party head-quarters, not in the streets. But the excited throngs pressed on.

Police in riot gear met the demonstrators. Pinochet was still president of Chile. He was not planning to leave yet. In dispersing the crowds, the police fired tear gas, water cannons, and bullets. One man and a fourteen-year-old boy died.

Pinochet had very much wanted to win the plebiscite, and he had fully expected voters to back him. When that did not happen, he had been perfectly willing to fix the election to give himself eight more years in office. He was prepared to call out the troops

THE DICTATORSHIP

and declare a state of siege. But General Matthei, the air force commander and member of the junta, had already publicly accepted the results. The opposition and outside observers were not going to accept false returns. More moderate members of Pinochet's government convinced him that he had to follow the timetable he had himself set up in the constitution of 1980. According to that document, Chileans had the right to nominate and elect a president to lead their government, as well as senators and representatives to form Chile's first Congress in seventeen years.

Elections were set for December 14, 1989. That schedule gave the political parties fourteen months to organize, nominate candidates, and run campaigns. The newly elected government would take office March 11, 1990. Until that date, Pinochet remained in La Moneda as president of Chile.

Most of Chile's political parties had not entirely disbanded, even when forced underground by junta decrees. In the months before the plebiscite, they gained members and strength. The Christian Democrats, the Socialists, and fourteen other smaller groups that had joined forces to campaign for "no" votes decided to stay allied for the presidential and congressional elections. The Concertación (agreement) for "No" became the Concertación for Democracy.

PARTIES AND COALITIONS

According to the ancient Greek philosopher Aristotle, "Man is a political animal." This is particularly evident in Chile. Politics is so popular there that, as a Chilean joke has it, if two Chileans are in a room, they represent at least three political parties. When the ban on political parties was finally lifted in the 1980s, Chileans quickly formed a wide variety of political groupings. Some, like the Christian Democrats and the Socialists, had existed before the coup. Others, such as the National Renewal Party, were old parties with fresh names. A few, such as the Humanists, were completely new.

To defeat Pinochet in 1988, the parties worked together. Their success showed the value of joining together in a common cause. In the twenty-first century, most parties participate in one of three coalitions: two major ones, the Concertación and the Alianza por Chile (Alliance for Chile), and the much smaller Juntos Podemos Más (Together We Can Do More). When asked, most Chileans identify with particular parties, not the larger coalitions.

This center-left alliance put together a list of common goals. They selected Patricio Aylwin, the president of the Christian Democratic Party, as their candidate for president. Aylwin was already well known to Chileans because he had acted as spokesperson for the Concertación for "No."

The right had splintered during the dictatorship. Some who had originally backed the coup grew less happy with prolonged military rule. Others wholeheartedly backed Pinochet. Two main groups formed before the elections—the traditional conservative party, called the National Renewal Party (RN, Renovación Nacional), and the pro-Pinochet Independent Democratic Union (UDI, Unión Demócrata Independiente). The two agreed to support one candidate for president, Hernán Büchi, a former finance minister in Pinochet's regime. Büchi had helped pull Chile out of the economic

PATRICIO AYLWIN PROMISES TO CONFRONT HUMAN RIGHTS ABUSES IN CHILE
in a speech during the 1989 election.

recession of the mid-1980s. The right-wing parties could not agree on congressional candidates, however, and weakened their chances of success by fielding five different congressional slates.

A third, independent candidate also competed for the presidency. Francisco Javier Errázuriz, a wealthy right-wing businessman, called himself a "man of the center."

NEGOTIATING DEMOCRACY

More difficult than organizing for the election was the struggle to return Chile to democratic rule. The purpose of Pinochet's constitution of 1980 was to give legal support to Pinochet's dictatorship. It was not at all useful as a guide for representative government. Especially undemocratic was the large proportion of appointed senators and the military control of the National Security Council. The constitution also left Pinochet in command of a very powerful army until 1998.

Except for the UDI leaders, who remained loyal to Pinochet, all the politicians wanted to make the constitution more democratic. Pinochet appointed Carlos Cáceres, his minister of the interior, to negotiate with the Concertación and the National Renewal Party on constitutional issues. Fifty-four changes were finally agreed on. One of them modified the National Security Council so that the military members no longer had the majority. Its role in the government became just advisory. To lessen the influence of the nine appointed senators, the number of elected senators was increased to thirty-eight. The ban on any political party that believed in the idea of class conflict (which had outlawed the Communist Party) was lifted. Procedures for amending the constitution were also simplified.

To encourage more people to take part in politics, another amendment gave unions and community organizations the freedom to participate in the political process. The reforms also reduced the power of the president to declare states of exception and forbade the use of exile as a punishment. In July 1989, Chileans voted on the package of reforms to the constitution. The revisions passed with 86 percent approval.

Many issues, however, remained unresolved. Pinochet had insisted on reducing the president's term of office to four years instead of eight, with no option for reelection. The opposition yielded to this demand, but only for the first post-Pinochet president.

A bigger problem for the democratic process was the system for electing members of Congress. According to this system, each of the nineteen senatorial districts elects two senators and each of the sixty deputorial districts elects two representatives. One party, however, can only win both seats in a district for the Senate or the Chamber of Deputies if the total of votes for them is more than two-thirds of the total vote in that district. This means that a minority party can win one seat with only 33.4 percent of the vote. But a majority party needs 66.7 percent of the vote to gain both seats. In this system, it would be possible for a minority party to win half the seats in the Congress with only a little more than a third of the votes. Since a minority of Chileans supported Pinochet in the plebiscite, this system was devised to favor Pinochet supporters.

With seventeen months from the plebiscite to the inauguration of the new government, Pinochet also had time to pass other laws to block democratization and make certain that his influence in the government would last as long as possible. An armed forces law prevented the military from being put under civilian rule. The Pinochet law gave commanders of each branch of the military control over appointments, retirements, and the military budget. A law also securely funded the military budget. Ten percent of the gross revenues of the state-owned copper company went to support the military.

Pinochet also offered bonuses to older justices of the Supreme Court who agreed to retire, so that he could appoint younger conservative justices to succeed them. Eight of the ten who were over seventy-five years old accepted Pinochet's offer.

Two other obstacles stood in the way of restoring justice to Chile. The democratic opposition was unable to revoke the amnesty law of 1978, and Pinochet refused to step down from his command of the army. When a journalist asked him why he wanted to remain commander in chief, Pinochet was perfectly frank. He wanted to make sure that the officers who had carried out his orders would not be tried for their crimes. "I have people in the army who could be ill-treated. I know that when politicians get into problems, they always make a double standard: 'It's not our fault,' they say. 'The law demands it.' . . . I tell you that my people are not going to be touched and that's that." With a large, well-armed, and loyal army backing him up, Pinochet assumed he could protect himself and his men from prosecution.

The election on December 14, 1989, gave a solid victory to the Concertación. Patricio Aylwin won an absolute majority with 55 percent of the vote. The Concertación captured 72 of the 120 seats in the Chamber of Deputies and twenty-two of the thirty-eight elective Senate positions. But it was not enough to dominate the Senate. The nine appointed senators were likely to vote with the elected right-wing senators to still give them a majority in the Senate.

On March 10, 1990, Pinochet delivered a farewell speech before ceremoniously leaving La Moneda. Asked by a reporter about his personal feelings on leaving the presidency, the departing dictator replied, "My feelings or those of anyone else have no importance to the greatness of Chile. What concerns me most is the country."

Pinochet's answer was less high minded when the reporter went on to ask how he would deal with the campaign against him and the military for human rights abuses. "I will keep silent because you have to let dogs bark. How could you think I would argue with lower class scandal sheets and the filth that is printed every week, and I am referring to certain magazines that—aren't they veritable sewers? . . . I can't sink to that level."

Two days later, Patricio Aylwin delivered his inaugural address at the National Stadium. Allende had spoken there twenty years earlier, after his inauguration. Many of those attending also remembered that prisoners had been detained, tortured, and killed there after the coup.

AN HONOR GUARD OF CHILEAN SOLDIERS STANDS AT ATTENTION AS
Patricio Aylwin, wearing the red, white, and blue sash of the president, arrives at the National Stadium in March 1990 to give his inaugural address.

"From this spot," Aylwin declared, "which in the sad days of blind and hateful dominance of force over reason, was for many a place of prison and torture, we say to all Chileans and to the world that is watching us: Never again!" Aylwin warned, however, that the return to civilian rule would only be partial owing to the "many limitations" and "obstacles" that Pinochet left behind.

In April, Aylwin made a courageous choice. Justice might be beyond his reach, but truth was not. He appointed a commission

NATIONAL TRUTH AND RECONCILIATION COMMISSION

The National Commission for Truth and Reconciliation was charged with the task of gathering all the evidence possible of human rights abuses between September 11, 1973, and March 11, 1990. The violations to be examined included both those committed by agents of the military regime and those committed by private persons for political purposes. The goal was to document what happened so that the government could begin to seek ways to make reparations and to prevent such atrocities from ever occurring again.

The eight-member commission, evenly divided between Pinochet supporters and the opposition, worked for nine months with a staff of sixty lawyers. In March 1991, it issued a six-volume, two-thousand-page report documenting 2,025 deaths and disappearances (a later investigation raised that total to 3,197). Only the victims were identified by name. All the evidence gathered was turned over to the courts for further investigations or legal actions.

to investigate and write a report on the massive abuses of the Pinochet dictatorship. Known as the National Commission for Truth and Reconciliation, it consisted of eight members from across the political spectrum. Raúl Rettig, a former Radical Party senator and respected jurist, chaired the commission.

Pinochet was angered by Aylwin's action and tried to stop civilians who had worked with the military regime from participating. His own "recipe for reconciliation," he told reporters, was simple: "Don't ask if the burning wood is oak, or walnut, or pine,

Chile's commission has served as a model for other transitions from repressive regimes to democratic governments. In 1995 it inspired the similar commission set up by President Nelson Mandela at the end of apartheid in South Africa.

In 1998 120 nations signed a treaty in Rome, Italy, to establish a court with the power to prosecute serious crimes of international concern, such as genocide, war crimes, and human rights abuses, when the country where the crimes were committed failed to act. (The United States voted against the treaty on the grounds that it did not exempt military officials from prosecution and as of 2008 has refused to sign it.) After the treaty was ratified by sixty countries (the number required by the treaty), the International Criminal Court (ICC) was established in the Netherlands at The Hague on July 1, 2002. Its jurisdiction extends to offenses committed after July 1, 2002, and committed in a nation that has ratified the agreement or by a citizen of such a nation. In all, some 140 nations have ratified the agreement.

or eucalyptus; just throw a bucket of water on the bonfire—and the problem is over! It must be forgotten!" He added: "Otherwise it becomes a Ping-Pong game, first on one side, then on the other, to infinity. Just cut it off with one stroke."

In September, Aylwin took another bold step toward rectifying the past by honoring Allende with a state funeral. Thousands of people turned out to see the procession from Viña del Mar, where the former president had been hastily buried after the coup, to the General Cemetery in Santiago. It was a moment of "reparation and reconciliation," Allende's widow said.

Work also began on a memorial to the victims of Pinochet's dic-

HORTENSIA BUSSI PAYS HER FINAL RESPECTS AT THE STATE FUNERAL for Salvador Allende in 1990. Thousands of Chileans joined Allende's family members at the ceremony.

tatorship, at the same cemetery. White marble panels 180 feet (55 m) long and 20 feet (6 m) high rest atop massive boulders. Engraved in the stone are the more than three thousand names of those who were arrested and disappeared or were executed for their political beliefs by the military regime. Next to their names are their ages and the dates they were detained or murdered. A different sort of memorial, the Park for Peace, was created at the Villa Grimaldi, one of the notorious torture centers operated by the DINA.

While Aylwin and the Concertación government worked to maintain Chile's prosperity and strengthen the civilian government, Pinochet wrote his memoirs, which he published in four books between 1990 and 1994. He kept up with politics, however, and threatened to mobilize the army to protest government activities he disapproved of.

In December 1990, the Chamber of Deputies began to investigate payments of nearly three million dollars the army made to Pinochet's son Augusto just before Pinochet left office. In retaliation, Pinochet called up the army, without notifying or explaining his actions to the department of defense. The government feared he planned to surround La Moneda with tanks, dismiss Congress, and call for new elections. After a tense night of negotiations, the investigation of Pinochet's son was shelved. The military call-up was officially explained as just an exercise.

Meanwhile, information about crimes committed during the military regime was growing. The eight members of the Commission for Truth and Reconciliation traveled up and down the country and even outside Chile. They interviewed victims and their families, searched the archives of humanitarian organizations, and took testimony from public and private agencies, including the military. Physical evidence was also turning up. In 1990 nineteen bodies buried soon after the coup were discovered at Pisagua. Then the remains of thirteen of the victims murdered in Calama in October 1973 were located in the Atacama Desert.

Six months after the publication of the Truth and Reconciliation report in March 1991, 126 more bodies of the disappeared were found. They had been buried in 108 coffins in Santiago's General Cemetery. The graves were marked "NN," perhaps for *ningún nombre* (no name). When a reporter asked if he knew that in some cases two bodies were found in a single coffin, Pinochet made light of the incident. "How very economical!" he said.

AN INTERNATIONAL CASE

Aylwin's four-year term ended in 1994, and he passed the presidential sash to his fellow Christian Democrat, Eduardo Frei, the son of the president before Allende. The Concertación had again won an absolute majority. Chileans hoped the new government would take further steps toward democracy. As one writer commented, the new president "still had a long road ahead, and he had to undertake it with a fully loaded backpack, in fact, an overloaded one."

As army commander, Pinochet remained the fierce protector of his family, the military, and his reputation. When a government agency attempted to reopen the case concerning the funds paid by the army to Pinochet's son Augusto, Pinochet again bullied the civilian government. This time President Frei closed the investigation entirely.

The government of Chile was caught trying to balance on a tightrope between democracy and the powerful remnants of the dictatorship it was trying to replace. "What we have today is not an imperfect democracy; rather is it an imperfect dictatorship," a diplomat quipped.

In Spain, however, Joan Garcés, a Spanish lawyer who had been an aide to Allende, was building an unprecedented legal case. He wanted a Spanish court to charge Pinochet with international terrorism and crimes against humanity. If the charges were to come to trial, it would be the first time that an ousted dictator was tried outside his own country for crimes committed by his regime. It would send the message that "no one is above international law, even when national laws protect you from prosecution."

In 1996 Spanish judge Baltasar Garzón agreed to take on the case that Garcés had presented to him for the families of some of Pinochet's victims. Lawyers began gathering depositions and assembling evidence, some of it provided by the findings of Chile's Commission for Truth and Reconciliation. There was one difficulty, however. Spanish law required that the accused be present at the trial. Pinochet would have to be taken to Spain. Chile and Spain had an extradition treaty (an agreement between two countries to surrender up alleged criminals for trial). But it was highly unlikely that Pinochet-appointed judges would rule in favor of his extradition.

GENERAL NO MORE

In March 1998, Pinochet's term as commander in chief of the army finally ended. In a ceremony at the military school where six decades earlier he had trained as a soldier, Pinochet handed over his ceremonial sword of office to his successor. The new commander, selected by President Frei from five generals eligible for the post, was a friend of Pinochet's. But he was the youngest of the group and had not played a political role in Pinochet's dictatorship, nor had he been accused of human rights violations.

The next day, dressed in a business suit, Pinochet rode through crowds of protesters to Valparaíso, where he had erected a new building for Congress, well away from the rest of the government in Santiago. There, sworn in as senator for life, he joined the senators he had appointed. His presence added one more unelected conservative vote to "protect" Chile from popular democracy. While his supporters applauded, some members of the opposition sat in silence, wearing black armbands and holding up photographs of victims of Pinochet's dictatorship.

Among those present that day were Allende's daughter Isabel

REPORTERS APPROACH PINOCHET *(CENTER)* **AS HE ARRIVES AT THE CHILEAN** congress in 1998 for his first session as a senator.

and Juan Pablo Letelier, whose father was assassinated at Pinochet's order. Both were members of Congress. The president of the Association of Families of the Detained and Disappeared said she felt "shame, rage, and impotence" at seeing the ousted dictator taking a role in Chile's restored democracy.

The year 1998 marked the twenty-fifth anniversary of the coup. As had been the case since 1974, September 11 was a national holiday. Several senators wanted to abolish the holiday but could never round up enough votes to do so. Pinochet took advantage of the situation to play the role of conciliator. He negotiated a compromise with the president of the Senate, Andrés Zaldívar, a Christian Democrat he had once sent into exile. Pinochet proposed to replace the holiday by a new holiday, a Day of National Unity, to be held on the first Monday of every September, beginning in 1999. The measure passed and was a public relations coup for Pinochet.

The approaching anniversary brought a flurry of publications about Allende's overthrow. The most sensational was a book called *Secret Interference* by Patricia Verdugo, a Chilean journalist. It is an annotated transcript of the radio communications among the officers of the junta during the attack on La Moneda. Accompanying the book is a CD of the conversations of the coup leaders that was secretly recorded by the radio operators. With its shocking revelations of the harsh language and grisly humor of the coup plotters, the book was an instant best seller.

Shortly after the commemorations of the twenty-fifth anniversary of the coup, the Pinochets and their eldest daughter, Lucía, took a trip to London, U.K., where Pinochet had arranged to undergo back surgery. He traveled on a diplomatic passport at the expense of Chile's government, and he would be paid a large commission by the Chilean army for signing an arms deal while there. On October

16, at a clinic in London, however, as Pinochet was recovering from the operation, two detectives from London's police service, Scotland Yard, served notice that he was under arrest. Great Britain was honoring Spain's request for extradition.

FIGHTING EXTRADITION

The news of Pinochet's arrest flashed around the world. In Santiago anti-Pinochet demonstrators rejoiced in the streets. Pinochet sup-

POLICE OUTSIDE THE BRITISH EMBASSY IN SANTIAGO FIRE A WATER CANNON at demonstrators protesting Pinochet's arrest.

porters stormed the British and Spanish embassies with such violence that police used water cannons to break up the demonstrations. Pinochet's backers organized a television marathon (a *Pinochetón*, they called it) to raise money to hire lawyers to fight Pinochet's extradition to Spain. Some women sold their jewels to make donations for his defense.

Pinochet spent sixteen months under house arrest in London while lawyers argued his case. At first, three judges ruled in favor of Pinochet, but they allowed for an appeal. The case then went to the House of Lords, the highest court of appeal in Great Britain. In November five law lords (a group of judges or lawyers who are members of the House of Lords) heard the case. The principal issue was whether a former head of state could be prosecuted for acts committed when he was head of state. In a 3–2 vote, the lords ruled that yes, Pinochet could be prosecuted for his crimes. In December the British government approved the extradition order. But Pinochet's lawyers objected to the decision on the grounds that one of the judges had a conflict of interest. He had helped raise funds for the human rights organization Amnesty International. The House of Lords then declared the decision of the law lords invalid. In January a group of seven different law lords heard the case. On March 24, 1999, the law lords ruled 6–1 that Pinochet could be extradited to Spain.

Pinochet's lawyers then challenged the validity of the extradition process. Former British prime minister Margaret Thatcher, meanwhile, led a public campaign to have Pinochet freed, claiming he was a "political prisoner" whose rights were being violated. In October a court ruled the extradition was valid.

Pinochet was confined to his rented house outside London. The Pinochet Foundation, started by his backers, paid the sixteen thousand dollars a month in rent. Although Thatcher and supporters from Chile came to visit, Pinochet's morale sank in the tedium of enforced exile. His physician reported he suffered two minor strokes. He had diabetes and kidney ailments too. But he did not want to be freed because of illness. He wanted his name cleared from the accusations he insisted were lies. It took many weeks for his lawyers to persuade him to undergo medical tests. On January 5, 2000, four doctors examined Pinochet for six hours and sent their report to the British home secretary Jack Straw, who had the power to release Pinochet for medical reasons.

Spain, Belgium, and other countries that also wanted to try Pinochet for human rights violations requested the results of the medical tests. More time passed while courts decided whether to approve sending the results abroad. But the final word about whether Pinochet would actually be sent to trial rested with Jack Straw, and on March 2, 2000, he ruled that Pinochet should be freed for "humanitarian reasons." On March 3, Pinochet arrived back in Chile.

Pinochet was lowered from the airplane in a wheelchair. When he reached the red carpet spread out on the tarmac, however, he rose from the wheelchair and strode toward the cheering supporters who had come to welcome him. Turning and waving his cane to show he did not need it, he smiled slyly at the television cameras. Back in Chile, he felt safe enough from prosecution to enjoy this

PINOCHET ARRIVES IN SANTIAGO

after sixteen months of detention in London.

little joke. He had fooled the British doctors and escaped the Spanish courts.

But Chile had changed. Pinochet's long absence had moved Chile farther along the road to recovery from dictatorship. In August 1999, military leaders sat down with human rights lawyers, civilian leaders, and the clergy for a *mesa de dialogo* (roundtable dialogue) about the disappeared. Over ten months of discussions, the twenty-two participants worked out legal measures to help locate the remains of the missing or at least to find out what had happened to them. For the first time, the armed forces acknowledged that human rights abuses had occurred, and they promised to gather information for the courts.

Also, while Pinochet was away, Chileans had once again exercised their democratic right to vote. For the first time since he left the presidency, Pinochet had not been an issue in the presidential elections. With Pinochet in England, the candidates running for president and Congress in Chile simply ignored the former dictator. They looked ahead, not back. In a close race, the candidate for the Concertación, the Socialist Ricardo Lagos, won the presidency. He was the first Socialist president of Chile since Allende.

On March 11, 2000, Lagos was inaugurated president of Chile. In his policy address the next day he pledged to rid the constitution of nondemocratic articles and complete the transition from dictatorship to democracy. Three months later, on June 26, 2000, to mark the ninety-second anniversary of Allende's birth, a statue of him was unveiled in front of La Moneda.

DODGING THE LAW

While Pinochet was in England, the number of cases brought against him and other members of the military regime had multiplied quickly. Three days after Pinochet returned, Judge Juan Guzmán of the Santiago Court of Appeals, who had been preparing a case against him, asked the Chilean courts to strip Pinochet of his legal immunity, which he held as a senator. The court did, and the Supreme Court upheld the decision. When charges were brought against Pinochet for authorizing the Caravan of Death, however, Pinochet's lawyers argued that Pinochet was too mentally infirm to stand trial.

For more than a year, the lawyers and the judge argued. According to Chilean law, Pinochet could only be released from trial if he were insane or suffered from dementia, but Pinochet refused to admit to either. So his lawyers argued that he was too frail physically to stand trial. When the judge agreed to have him physically examined, there were further delays and evasions. At last doctors found a slight vascular dementia (intellectual deterioration) from the strokes Pinochet had suffered, and the lawyers seized that phrase to prove he was unfit.

The government did not openly take sides in the struggle. The

Court of Appeals went along with the lawyers and voted to suspend the case concerning the Caravan of Death for reasons of Pinochet's health. The Supreme Court upheld that decision on July 1, 2002. Many people were angry that Pinochet escaped justice. Pinochet's victory was not total, however. If he was too mentally unfit to be tried, how could he serve in the Senate?

Aware that he might be facing another ouster, Pinochet sent a letter resigning his position as senator for life. He remained proud of himself and his dictatorship in spite of all the evidence and charges against him. "I have a clean conscience," he wrote. "I have hope that in the future my soldierly sacrifice will be valued and recognized. The work of my government will be judged by history."

Pinochet was free, but he could not travel outside Chile without fear of arrest. Spain had declared him a fugitive from justice. Nor did he find a friendly welcome when he went for a vacation in Iquique. There, his bodyguards arrested teenagers with toy water guns at the beach, and their parents threatened legal action. Pinochet fled back to Santiago. He became increasingly isolated in his fortified family compounds, traveling between them with bodyguards in armored cars.

THE JUDGMENT OF HISTORY

Pinochet's escape from justice did not stop the investigations into the crimes of his dictatorship. Judge Guzmán was a tenacious investigator and prosecutor. To get around the amnesty law, he focused on crimes committed after 1978 and on disappearances. He justified this on the legal grounds that if no body had been found, the crime was ongoing.

In 2002 a CNI hit man was given life imprisonment for assassinating a union leader in 1982. An air force general was arrested for obstructing justice by destroying evidence concerning eleven hundred disappeared Chileans. One of Pinochet's bodyguards was indicted in the murder of a defecting DINA agent. The following year, Pinochet's head of the DINA, General Manuel Contreras, was convicted of atrocities committed at Villa Grimaldi. Together with his deputy, Contreras was also indicted for his role in the assassination of General Prats. The courts were filled with several hundred cases against former military officers.

In August 2003, President Lagos assigned an eight-member National Commission on Political Imprisonment and Torture to investigate all cases of torture that occurred between September 11, 1973, and March 11, 1990. The commission spent a year interviewing tens of thousands of victims. In November 2004, its report confirmed twenty-eight thousand cases of torture and detailed the shocking methods used. The report made clear that torture was not the occasional "excess" that Pinochet partisans often claimed. It was widespread and systematic, an integral part of Pinochet's dictatorship.

The same year, Pinochet's supporters received another bombshell revelation about their hero. The man they had raised money to help—establishing a foundation in his name and paying for top British legal help—had millions of dollars in secret bank accounts outside Chile. Even one of Pinochet's closest military colleagues expressed surprise. As investigators turned their attention to the bank accounts, they discovered millions more dollars in accounts under various family names, as well as several aliases. At least twenty-eight million dollars was found at eight banks that operate in the United States.

> *"The Army of Chile has taken the difficult but irreversible decision to assume the responsibility for all punishable and morally unacceptable acts in the past that fall on it as an institution. Never and for no one can there be any ethical justification for human rights violations."*
>
> —General Juan Emilio Cheyre, commander in chief of the Chilean army, November 2004

Meanwhile, Guzmán did not give up prosecuting Pinochet. In December 2004, the Supreme Court decided that he was fit to stand trial and indicted him on charges related to Operation Condor. Pinochet was briefly back under house arrest while his lawyers appealed. In November 2005, he was charged in another case of torture and killings. In early 2006, his wife and four grown children were arrested for tax evasion and fraud. His daughter Lucía fled by car to Argentina and flew to the United States to ask for asylum, but she was denied entry and returned to face arrest in Chile.

In 2006 new evidence turned up showing that Pinochet's crimes continued after his dictatorship. As commander in chief of the army between 1990 and 1998, Pinochet presided over several illegal enterprises. They were the likely source of the money discovered in the foreign bank accounts. According to charges made by former associates, an army chemical plant was used to manufacture cocaine. The cocaine was smuggled out of Chile and transported to Europe and the United States for sale. In addition, a ring of high-ranking military officers was charged with illegal arms sales that violated Chilean treaties and UN embargos. The disappearance of a secret police chemist in 1991 and an army colonel in 1992 have been linked to these illicit businesses. The colonel disappeared before he could give evidence about the covert arms deals. When the bodies of these men were later recovered, forensic evidence indicated they had been murdered.

Pinochet had a heart attack in early December 2006. Although at first the prognosis for recovery was good, he died on December 10. He was ninety-one years old. At the time of his death, he was being tried for tax evasion, tax fraud, falsification of official documents, and the use of fake passports. He had been indicted in three human rights cases and was the subject of dozens of judicial inquiries.

It is too early to know how history will judge Augusto Pinochet. The investigations and indictments continue as the courts sort out the various crimes of his dictatorship. To the end, he pictured himself as Chile's savior from totalitarian rule. His supporters credit him with modernizing Chile and bringing prosperity to many Chileans. The president of the Pinochet Foundation spoke to reporters outside the hospital after Pinochet's death. "Pinochet rescued and transformed Chile into the country we all feel proud of," he said. "Once passions subdue, he will be given his place in history as architect of our nation."

But the majority of Chileans consider him a dark blot on Chile's history. As the director of Human Rights Watch Americas, José Miguel Vivanco pointed out, "Pinochet spent his last years fending off an ever-tightening web of prosecutions in Chile and died a profoundly discredited figure in the land he once ruled." Many Chileans rejoiced that he was finally gone. Isabel Letelier,

POETIC JUSTICE

In January 2006, Michelle Bachelet was elected the first woman president of Chile. She received more than 53 percent of the vote. Like many Chileans, she suffered during Pinochet's dictatorship. Her father, an air force general, was tortured and died following a heart attack while in military custody in 1974. She and her mother were also detained and tortured and later fled into exile. "Violence ravaged my life," Bachelet said in her victory speech when she was elected. "I was a victim of hatred, and I have dedicated my life to reversing that hatred." A candidate of the Concertación, she is a Socialist. "But," she told an interviewer, "I will be president for all the Chileans." She is optimistic that Chile will continue its progress as a stable democracy.

the widow of Orlando Letelier, however, expressed the disappointment many families of victims felt. "I was not happy," she said in a radio interview. "I was appalled that he had died without being sentenced. . . . I hope that [he] will be remembered [for what he was]: a coward, criminal, and thief."

WHO'S WHO?

ISABEL ALLENDE (B. 1945): The youngest daughter of Salvador Allende, Isabel Allende was a sociologist active in the women's movement during her father's administration. (Her cousin, also named Isabel Allende, is a famous writer.) After the coup, she accompanied her sister Beatriz into exile in Havana, Cuba, and later traveled around Europe, Africa, and Australia speaking out for the restoration of democracy in Chile. She settled for a time in Mexico, where her mother was also living in exile, then returned to Chile with her husband and two children in 1988. She won a seat in the Chamber of Deputies in 1993. While Pinochet was under arrest in London, she flew there to present a letter to the government urging Pinochet's extradition to Spain. She has continued to serve in Congress as a member of the Socialist Party.

PATRICIO AYLWIN (B. 1918): A professor of administrative law and a respected lawyer, Patricio Aylwin is the son of a judge who became president of the Supreme Court. In 1951 Patricio became president of the National Falange. He helped found the Christian Democratic Party in 1957. He served in the Senate from 1965 to 1973 and opposed many UP programs during Allende's presidency. Aylwin welcomed the coup in 1973 but was soon disillusioned. When he won the presidential election in 1989, he gave high priority to exposing the human rights violations of Pinochet's dictatorship.

MICHELLE BACHELET (B. 1951): The daughter of an air force officer and an archaeologist, Michelle Bachelet spent her preteen years in Washington, D.C., where her father was assigned to the military mission at the Chilean Embassy. Later, she studied medicine at the University of Chile and became active in the Socialist Party. After the coup, her father was imprisoned and tortured before dying following a heart attack. She and her mother were tortured and exiled. After returning to Chile in 1979, she completed her degree in pediatrics and public health and began practicing medicine. In 1996 she enrolled in Chile's National War College to study strategy and defense. President Richard Lagos appointed her health minister in 2000 and, two years later, defense minister, the first woman in Latin American history to hold that post. In January 2006, she was elected as the first woman president in Chilean history.

MANUEL CONTRERAS (B. 1929): Known as Mamo, Contreras grew up in a middle-class military family and attended the military school when Pinochet, then a captain, was teaching there. In the late 1960s, Contreras spent two years at the U.S. Army Career Officers School in Fort Belvoir, Virginia. Like Pinochet, Contreras built a loyal following among younger officers. In 1973 he was given command of the Army School of Engineers at Tejas Verdes in San Antonio, the port closest to Santiago. After the coup, he arrested UP militants and sympathizers and set up detention centers. Pinochet soon made him director of DINA. Contreras was also involved in organizing Operation Condor. When Pinochet disbanded DINA in 1977, he promoted Contreras to general and made him chief of security. Contreras was among the first of the military regime to be convicted of human rights crimes. The accumulated sentences for the many cases for which he has been tried, as of September 2007, add up to 224 years, and cases against him are still being heard in 2008. He has written a book titled *Historical Truth* giving his version of the coup.

HARALD EDELSTAM (1913–1989): The Swedish diplomat Harald Edelstam became known for his courage in defying military authorities during World War II, when he helped hundreds of Norwegian refugees escape from the Nazis. As ambassador to Chile at the time of the coup, he used his own diplomatic immunity to face down military officers and help UP sympathizers avoid arrest. Besides rescuing the Cuban Embassy, he went to the National Stadium and personally persuaded officers to release many detainees, among them forty Uruguayans scheduled for execution. Using disguises, false names, and forged documents, he aided the departure of many leftists from Chile. He smuggled refugees to asylum in his own embassy as well as those of Mexico, Costa Rica, Venezuela, and Finland. He also saw to it that film footage of the military coup left the country with his diplomatic mail so that the rest of the world could witness events in Chile. In December 1973, the junta ordered him out of the country.

JOAN GARCÉS (B. 1944): A Spaniard from Valencia, Garcés first went to Chile as a graduate student in the 1960s. He became a trusted aide to Salvador Allende and was in La Moneda with the president during the coup. Allende ordered him to leave, saying "Someone has to relate what has happened here, and only you can do that." Garcés escaped from the building and managed to get back to Spain. There he started the Salvador Allende Foundation and wrote several books about Chile. For many years, he practiced law in Madrid. The idea of bringing Pinochet to justice in Spain struck him when he read that a Spanish court was prosecuting former members of Argentina's military junta. Although disappointed that his work did not bring Pinochet to trial, he was proud of having made the effort. "What is important is that he died under international warrants by the courts of justices of several countries. . . . So he died as a fugitive of justice."

RICARDO LAGOS (B. 1938): Lagos's father, a farmworker, died when Ricardo was eight. Lagos studied law at the University of Chile and earned a Ph.D. in economics from Duke University in Durham, North Carolina. He returned and taught economics at the University of Chile, becoming its rector from 1971 to 1972. In 1971 Allende named him Chile's ambassador to the UN. After the coup, Lagos and his wife and children sought asylum in Argentina. He taught in Buenos Aires and at Duke. He returned to Chile in 1978 to work for the UN Latin American Employment program. He became active in politics and was accused of playing a role in the Pinochet assassination attempt. He was later freed and the charges dropped. During the transition to democracy, he served as Aylwin's education minister and later Frei's public works minister. In 1999 Lagos was elected president. He introduced a variety of social legislation while improving Chile's economic growth. He appointed a commission to report on torture during the regime and allowed the courts to prosecute cases against the military.

MÓNICA MADARIAGA (B. 1942): A brilliant lawyer who was a second cousin of Augusto Pinochet, Madariaga became Pinochet's legal adviser after the coup. As Pinochet's minister of justice (1977–1983), Madariaga drafted the infamous Decree 2191, granting amnesty to all politically motivated crimes between the coup and 1978. She also helped design the "protected" democracy of the constitution of 1980. She made many enemies among the military during a brief eight-month tenure as minister of education in 1983. She later claimed that she only became aware of the atrocities of the dictatorship "through faxes I received as president of the Organization of American States." In spite of her differences with the dictatorship, she defends her cousin Pinochet as a great leader of Chile.

RAÚL RETTIG (1909–2000): A lawyer, teacher, ambassador, senator, and cabinet member, Rettig joined the centrist Radical Party in his youth and remained actively involved in it all his life. He first ran for Congress in 1937 and served both as a deputy and as a senator. A fiery speaker, he once engaged in such a heated argument with his fellow senator, the Socialist Salvador Allende, that he challenged Allende to a duel. The two met at dawn with pistols. Both fired, but made certain they missed. Their two parties later joined forces, with the Rettig's Radical Party supporting Allende's Popular Unity in 1970. During the military dictatorship, Rettig returned to practicing law privately, becoming president of the lawyer's association. Patricio Aylwin chose him to lead the Commission for Truth and Reconciliation in 1990 and later the Reparations and Reconciliation Commission which carried the investigations further in 1992.

RAÚL SILVA (1907–1999): As the archbishop of Santiago from 1961 to 1983, Silva became widely known for his charitable work on behalf of poor, oppressed, and homeless Chileans. During Allende's administration, he tried to avert the coup by bringing the Socialist and Christian Democratic leaders together. After the coup, he and Jewish and Protestant leaders organized the Committee for Peace to help victims and refugees of the military dictatorship. When Pinochet ordered the committee dissolved in 1975, Silva started the Vicariate of Solidarity, which protected opposition groups, gave legal aid to political prisoners, defended the lawyers who took on human rights cases, and kept records of human rights abuses. He retired when he turned seventy-five, and he wrote three volumes of memoirs detailing the church's work during the dictatorship.

TIMELINE

CA. 12,000–10,000 B.C.   The first humans settle in Chile.

A.D. 1541   Spanish conquistador Pedro de Valdivia founds Santiago.

1810–1818   Chile fights the War of Independence from Spain.

1879–1883   Chile gains mining territory from Peru and Bolivia in the War of the Pacific.

1891   The Chilean Congress defeats President Balmaceda in a brief civil war.

1915   Pinochet is born on November 25 in Valparaíso.

1931–1932   The worldwide Great Depression brings political turmoil to Chile. Two military juntas take over the government for brief periods.

1933   The Socialist Party is founded in Chile. Pinochet enters military school.

1970   Salvador Allende is elected the first Socialist president of Chile.

1971   Pinochet is promoted to major general and given command of the Santiago garrison.

1973   Pinochet is named army commander after General Prats resigns. Military and police leaders overthrow the Allende government.

1974   Pinochet persuades the three other junta members to sign Decree 527, making him the supreme chief of the nation (later changed to president).

1978 Pinochet issues Decree 2191, granting amnesty to people who committed politically motivated crimes between 1973 and 1978.

1980 Chileans vote for Pinochet's new constitution, in a plebiscite. An economic slump brings a growing opposition to Pinochet's dictatorship.

1988 A plebiscite is held to decide if Pinochet will remain president for a second eight-year term, and fifty-four percent of Chileans vote no.

1989 Democratic presidential and congressional elections are held. Patricio Aylwin wins the presidential race.

1990 Pinochet steps down as president. He remains commander in chief of the army.

1998 Pinochet steps down as commander in chief of the army and becomes senator for life. Pinochet is arrested in London on charges by a Spanish judge of terrorism and crimes against humanity.

2006 Michelle Bachelet is elected first woman president of Chile. Pinochet dies after a heart attack, on December 10.

GLOSSARY

capitalism: an economic system that allows private ownership of resources, industries, and the means to distribute goods. In a capitalist system, industries are controlled by the owner and the market, rather than the government.

CNI: Central Nacional de Informaciones (National Information Center); the information agency that replaced the DINA in 1977 to gather intelligence for the dictatorship and to continue the DINA's covert activities; like the DINA, directly controlled by Pinochet

Communism: a political and economic model based on the idea of common, rather than private, property. In a Communist system, the government controls capital and distributes it equally among citizens. The system is based on the writings of the German economist Karl Marx.

concertación: an agreement by diverse groups to work together (in concert) for a particular issue or candidate; a political alliance

curfew: a regulation requiring people to stay off the streets after a stated hour

DINA: Dirección de Inteligencia Nacional (National Intelligence Directorate); the secret police organization that began operation in November 1973, headed by Manuel Contreras and directly under Pinochet's control; replaced in 1977 by the CNI

disappeared: victims of a dictatorship who are arrested and secretly detained, tortured, executed, and disposed of, with all records of their arrest and murder destroyed or concealed

FPMR: Frente Patriótico Manuel Rodríguez (Manuel Rodríguez Patriotic Front); a guerrilla group named for a hero of Chile's War of Independence (1810–1818) and founded by the Communist Party in 1983 to oppose the military regime, mostly by bombing power lines and communications facilities. The group attempted to assassinate Pinochet in 1986.

FRAP: Frente de Acción Popular (Front for Popular Action); a coalition of leftist parties formed in 1956 that supported Allende's candidacy for president in 1958 and 1964

junta (HOON-tah): a committee formed for the purposes of temporarily governing a country during or following a period of unrest; members share power equally although one may lead meetings and act as spokesperson

minister: a high government official appointed to manage a division of government activities

ministry: a government department

MIR: Movimiento de Izquierda Revolucionaria (Movement of the Revolutionary Left); a guerrilla group founded in 1967 and patterned after Fidel Castro's guerrilla organization

Patria y Libertad: a right-wing guerrilla group founded in 1970 with CIA support to undermine Allende's presidency by economic sabotage and assassinations

Socialism: a social system in which the government controls and manages some part of the production and distribution of goods.

UP: Unidad Popular (Popular Unity); a coalition of six left-wing parties formed in 1969 to bring Socialism to Chile through democratic processes. It supported Allende's candidacy for president in 1970.

SELECTED BIBLIOGRAPHY

Arriagada, Genaro. *Pinochet: The Politics of Power.* Translated by Nancy Morris. Winchester, MA: Unwin Hyman, 1988.

Burbach, Roger. *The Pinochet Affair: State Terrorism and Global Justice.* London: Zed Books, 2003.

Chavkin, Samuel. *Storm over Chile: The Junta under Siege.* Westport, CT: Lawrence Hill, 1985.

Collier, Simon, and William F. Sater. *A History of Chile, 1802–2002.* 2nd ed. Cambridge: Cambridge University Press, 2004.

Comisión Nacional de Verdad y Reconciliación, Chile. *Report of the Chilean National Commission on Truth and Reconciliation.* Translated by Phillip E. Berryman. 2 vols. Notre Dame, IN: University of Notre Dame Press, 1993.

Constable, Pamela, and Arturo Valenzuela. *A Nation of Enemies: Chile under Pinochet.* New York: W. W. Norton & Co., 1991.

Davis, Nathaniel. *The Last Two Years of Salvador Allende.* Ithaca, NY: Cornell University Press, 1985.

Drake, Paul W., and Ivan Jaksic. *The Struggle for Democracy in Chile.* Rev. ed. Lincoln: University of Nebraska Press, 1995.

Ensalaco, Mark. *Chile under Pinochet: Recovering the Truth.* Philadelphia: University of Pennsylvania Press, 2000.

Hawkins, Darren G. *International Human Rights and Authoritarian Rule in Chile.* Lincoln: University of Nebraska Press, 2002.

Hickman, John. *News from the End of the Earth: A Portrait of Chile.* New York: St. Martin's Press, 1998.

Huneeus, Carlos. *The Pinochet Regime.* Translated by Lake Sagaris. Boulder, CO: Lynne Rienner, 2007.

Kornbluh, Peter. *The Pinochet File: A Declassified Dossier on Atrocity and Accountability*. New York: New Press, 2004.

Loveman, Brian. *Chile: The Legacy of Hispanic Capitalism*. 3rd ed. New York: Oxford University Press, 2001.

Oppenheim, Lois Hecht. *Politics in Chile: Socialism, Authoritarianism, and Market Democracy*. 3rd ed. Boulder, CO: Westview Press, 2007.

O'Shaughnessy, Hugh. *Pinochet: The Politics of Torture*. New York: New York University Press, 2000.

Pinochet Ugarte, Augusto. *Camino recorrido*. 3 vols. Santiago, Chile: Instituto Geográfico Militar de Chile, 1990–1994.

———. *El día decisivo: 11 de septiembre de 1973*. Santiago, Chile: Editorial Andrés Bello, 1979.

Politzer, Patricia. *Fear in Chile: Lives under Pinochet*. New York: New Press, 2001.

Sigmund, Paul E. *The United States and Democracy in Chile*. Baltimore: Johns Hopkins University Press, 1993.

Spooner, Mary Helen. *Soldiers in a Narrow Land: The Pinochet Regime in Chile*. Berkeley: University of California Press, 1994.

Timerman, Jacobo. *Chile: Death in the South*. Translated by Robert Cox. New York: Knopf, 1987.

Varas, Florencia, and José Manuel Vergara. *Coup! Allende's Last Day*. New York: Stein and Day, 1975.

Verdugo, Patricia. *Chile, Pinochet, and the Caravan of Death*. Translated by Marcelo Montecino. Coral Gables, FL: North-South Center Press, 2001.

———. *Interferencia secreta*. Santiago, Chile: Editorial Sudamericana, 1998.

White, Judy, ed. *Chile's Days of Terror: Eyewitness Accounts of the Military Coup*. New York: Pathfinder Press, 1974.

FURTHER READING, FILMS, AND WEBSITES

Allende, Isabel. *The House of Spirits*. Translated by Magda Bogin. New York: Knopf, 1985.

———. *My Invented Country, A Nostalgic Journey through Chile*. Translated by Margaret Sayers Peden. New York: Harper Collins, 2003.

DiPiazza, Francesca Davis. *Chile in Pictures.* Minneapolis: Twenty-First Century Books, 2007.

Dorfman, Ariel. *Chile, the Other September 11*. New York: Ocean Press, 2003.

———. *Death and the Maiden*. New York: Penguin, 1992.

Dwyer, Christopher. *Chile.* Philadelphia: Chelsea House, 1999.

Galvin, Irene. *Chile: Journey to Freedom*. Parsippany, NJ: Dillon Press, 1997.

Garza, Hedda. *Salvador Allende*. New York: Chelsea House, 1989.

FILMS

Machuca. DVD. Directed by Andrés Wood. Barcelona: Cameo Media, 2004.

Missing. DVD. Directed by Constantin Costa-Gavras. 1982; Universal City, CA: Universal Studios Home Video, 2004.

WEBSITES

Amnesty International Report on Chile
http://thereport.amnesty.org/eng/Regions/Americas/Chile
A worldwide movement of people who campaign for internationally recognized human rights to be respected and protected, Amnesty International posts annual reports online.

Derechos Chile (Human Rights in Chile)

http://www.chipsites.com/derechos/index_eng.html

A history of human rights abuses in Chile beginning in 1973, including testimony and photographs, is available at this site.

Human Rights Watch: Americas—Chile

http://hrw.org/doc/?t=americas&c=chile

This organization, dedicated to protecting human rights around the world, offers a collection of articles on Chile's progress in prosecuting the crimes and compensating the victims of the dictatorship as well as current issues about the rights of Mapuche people in Chile.

Isabel Allende Interview

http://www.amnesty.dk/default.asp?page=2822&lang=da

Amnesty International Denmark's site features an interview in English with the Chilean novelist. The occasion is the opening of a Swedish film *The Black Pimpernel*, a biopic about Harald Edelstam, the Swedish ambassador during the coup in Chile.

Memoria Viva (Living Memory)

http://www.memoriaviva.com/English.htm

Sponsored by Human Rights International, this nongovernmental organization was established by Chilean refugees and human rights activists in London. Its website hosts testimonies in Spanish and English from victims and perpetrators of human rights abuses in Chile.

Remember Chile

http://www.remember-chile.org.uk/index.htm

The website was created in 1998 in London by Chilean exiles and others concerned about human rights in Chile. It includes "Pinochet for Beginners," an introduction to the dictatorship; articles on "Inside the Dictatorship" and "Testimonies" from families of victims of the regime.

SOURCE NOTES

Note: All translations of Spanish texts are by the author unless otherwise indicated.

7 Patricia Verdugo, *Interferencia secreta* (Santiago, Chile: Editorial Sudamericana 1998), 103.

8 Ibid., 104.

8 Collier, 112.

8 Augusto Pinochet Ugarte, *Camino recorrido* (Santiago, Chile: Instituto Geografico Militar de Chile, 1991), 2:18.

10 Roger Burbach, *The Pinochet Affair:State Terrorism and Global Justice* (London: Zed Books, 2003), 36.

11 Simon Collier and William F. Sater, *A History of Chile, 1808–2002.* 2nd ed. (Cambridge: Cambridge Univ. Press, 2004), xix.

19 Ibid., 194.

21 *The Communist Manifesto and Other Revolutionary Writings*, Bob Blaisdell, ed. (Mineola, NY: Dover, 2003), 150.

22 Collier and Sater, 200.

26 Ibid., 216.

28 Pinochet, *Camino recorrido*, 1:36.

29 Hugh O'Shaughnessy, *Pinochet, the Politics of Torture* (New York: New York University Press, 2000), 11.

29 Pinochet, *Camino recorrido* 1:64.

29 Ibid.,1:89.

30 O'Shaughnessy, 26.

35 Collier and Sater, 290.

40 Pinochet, *El día decisivo* (Santiago, Chile: Editorial Andrés Bello, 1979), 42.

42 Peter Kornbluh, *The Pinochet File:A Declassified Dossier on Atrocity and Accountability* (New York: New Press, 2004), 17.

42 Ibid., 85.

44 Collier and Sater, 334.

47 Collier and Sater, 352.

49 O'Shaughnessy, 46.

49 Nathaniel Davis, *The Last Two Years of Salvador Allende* (Ithaca, NY: Cornell University Press, 1985), 164.

50 Burbach, 40.

51 O'Shaughnessy, 52.

56 Florencia Varas and José Manuel Vergara, *Coup! Allende's Last Day* (New York: Stein and Day, 1975), 51–53.

57 Pinochet, *Camino recorrido*, 2:18–19.

59 Genaro Arriagada, *Pinochet: The Politics of Power*, trans. Nancy Morris (Winchester.,MA: Unwin Hyman, 1988), 8.

59 Ibid., 9.

60 Judy White, ed., *Chile's Days of Terror: Eyewitness Accounts of the Military Coup* (New York: Pathfinder Press, 1974), 30–31.

63 Kevin G. Hall, "Chilean Torture Victims Demand Compensation, Prosecution," Knight-Ridder, December 13, 2004, http://www.commondreams.org/headlines04/1213-08.htm (April 23, 2008)

64 O'Shaughnessy, 79.

64 Ibid., 80.

64 Pamela Constable and Arturo Valenzuela, *A Nation of Enemies: Chile under Pinochet* (New York:
W. W. Norton, 1991), 65.

65 Collier and Sater, 361.

68 O'Shaughnessy, 123.

69 Collier and Sater, 364.

70 Constable and Valenzuela, 129.

72 Ibid., 73.

73 Arriagada, 54.

75 Ibid., 69.

76 Edward Schumacher, "Chile's Leader, Belittling Foes, Vows to Stay On," *New York Times*, August 8, 1984, A4.

76 Constable and Valenzuela, 76.

78 O'Shaughnessy, 122.

79 Constable and Valenzuela, 306.

80 Mary Helen Spooner, *Soldiers in a Narrow Land: The Pinochet Regime in Chile* (Berkeley: University of California Press, 1994), 241.

81 Constable and Valenzuela, 310.

85 White, 103.

86 Sheila Cassidy, *The Audacity to Believe* (London: Collins, 1977), 68.

86 Ibid.

86   Constable and Valenzuela, 146–147.

89   Jacopo Timerman, *Chile: Death in the South*, trans. Robert Cox (New York: Knopf, 1987), 12.

89   Ibid.

89   Ibid., 6.

90   Timerman, 17.

97   Constable and Valenzuela, 154.

98   Ibid., 160.

98   Ibid., 161.

99   Brian Loveman, *Chile: The Legacy of Hispanic Capitalism*, 3rd ed. (New York: Oxford University Press, 2001), 265.

99   Samuel Chavkin, *Storm over Chile: The Junta under Siege* (Westport, CT.: Lawrence Hill, 1985), 260.

99   Constable and Valenzuela, 157.

102 David Binder, "Chile's Junta Says It Kept U.S. In Dark," *New York Times,* September 15, 1973, 11.

102 "U.S. Had Warning Of Coup, Aides Say," *New York Times,* September 13, 1973, 18.

104 Kornbluh, 17.

104 Ibid., 115.

104 Ibid., 209.

104 Ibid., 213.

105 Ibid., 211.

106 Loveman, 271.

107 Paul E. Sigmund, *The United States and Democracy in Chile* (Baltimore: Johns Hopkins University Press, 1993), 105.

108 Arriagada, 35–36.

112 Samuel Chavkin, *Murder of Chile: Eyewitness Accounts of the Coup, the Terror, and the Resistance Today* (New York: Everest House, 1982), 265–66.

114 Sigmund, 149.

114 Ibid., 149.

116 Burbach, 78.

120 Collier and Sater, 381.

122 Pinochet, *Camino recorrido*, 3: 2, 291.

123 Pinochet, *Camino recorrido*, 3:2, 291.

123 Ibid.

124 Spooner, 256.

124 Kornbluh, 471.

126   Pinochet, *Camino recorrido*,
      3:2, 290.

126   Collier and Sater, 391.

128   Mark Ensalaco, *Chile under
      Pinochet: Recovering the Truth*
      (Philadelphia: University of
      Pennsylvania Press, 2000), 227.

128   Rafael Otano, *Crónica de la
      Transición* (Santiago, Chile:
      Planeta, 1995), 368.

128   O'Shaughnessy, 155.

129   Amnesty International, "The
      Pinochet Case," March 2, 2000,
      http://www.amnesty.org/ailib/
      intcam/pinochet/ (November
      12, 2007).

131   Viñas, Miguel Angel, "¡A sus
      órdenes, mi senador!" VHS
      (Princeton, NJ: Films for the
      Humanities and Sciences, 2001).

133   Collier and Sater, 407.

134   Burbach, 115.

134   Ibid., 122.

136   Ibid., 136.

137   Kornbluh, 490.

139   Larry Rohter, "Chile's Army
      Accepts Blame for Rights
      Abuses in the Pinochet Era,"
      New York Times, November 6,
      2004, A5.

140   Pascale Bonnefoy, "Joy,
      and Violence, at Death of
      Pinochet," *New York Times*,
      December 11, 2006, A8.

140   Ibid.

141   Larry Rohter, "A Leader
      Making Peace with Chile's
      Past," *New York Times*, January
      16, 2006.

141   "The Woman Taking Chile's
      Top Job," *BBC News*, January 16,
      2006, http://news.bbc.co.uk/
      2/hi/americas/4087510.stm
      (April 23, 2008).

141   "Pinochet's Chile," *Talk of the
      Nation*, National Public Radio,
      December 11, 2006.

144   Burbach, 18.

144   "Seven Questions: Joan Garcés
      on Pinochet's Death," *Foreign
      Policy,* December 2006, http://
      www.foreignpolicy.com/
      story/cms.php?story_id=3651
      (November 27, 2007).

145   Mónica Madariage, "TVN: De
      Pe a Pa," interviewed by Pedro
      Carcuro, October 11, 2004,
      http://www.tvn.cl/programas/
      depeapa/2003/detalle.asp
      ?id=300 (November 26, 2007).

INDEX

PHOTO ACKNOWLEDGMENTS

The images in this book are used with the permission of: © Robert Nickelsberg/Time & Life Pictures/Getty Images, p. 1; AP Photo/El Mercurio, p. 7; © Laura Westlund/Independent Picture Service, p. 9; Library of Congress, pp. 16 (LC-USZ62-44903), 23 (LC-USZ62-117884); The Granger Collection, New York, p. 18; © Hulton Archive/Getty Images, p. 26; © Keystone Pictures/ZUMA Press, p. 37; AP Photo, pp. 41, 45, 49, 53, 74, 84, 113; AP Photo/ja/cb, p. 46; © AFP/Getty Images, pp. 62, 110; AP Photo/ Di Baia, p. 64; © Bettmann/CORBIS, pp. 73, 101; © Alexis Duclos/Gamma/ Eyedea/ZUMA Press, p. 78; © Horacio Villalobos/CORBIS, p. 88; AP Photo/ Santiago Llanquin, pp. 93, 130, 132; © Greg Smith/CORBIS, p. 95; © STR/ AFP/Getty Images, p. 107; REUTERS/STR New, p. 115; © Julio Etchart/Impact Photos/ZUMA Press, p. 119; © Carlos Carrion/Sygma/CORBIS, p. 123; © Diego Goldberg/CORBIS, p. 126; AP Photo/Ricardo Mazalan, p. 135.

Front cover: © Robert Nickelsberg/Time Life Pictures/Getty Images (main); AP Photo/Eduardo Di Baia (background).

AUTHOR BIOGRAPHY

Diana Childress was born in Texas and grew up in Mexico City. She has a Ph.D. in medieval English literature and has taught college-level classes and been a school librarian in New York City, where she now lives. She is the author of *The War of 1812* (Chronicle of America's Wars), *George H. W. Bush* (Presidential Leaders), *Marco Polo's Journey to China* and *Johannes Gutenberg and the Printing Press* (Pivotal Moments in History), and a biography of Álvaro Nuñez Cabeza de Vaca, *Barefoot Conquistador,* as well as other books and articles for young readers.